JOHN MISTO has been writing for Australian stage and television for over two decades. His play, *The Shoe-Horn Sonata* won both the NSW Premier's Literary Award and the Australia Remembers National Play Competition. Misto also wrote a companion piece, a telemovie called *Sisters of War*, which won the Queensland Premier's Literary Award.

Misto's play, *Harp on the Willow* completed a sell-out season at the Ensemble Theatre in Sydney with Marina Prior in the starring role. *Harp* won the Rodney Seaborn Award for best New Play.

John Misto's television credits are extensive. He wrote *Heroes' Mountain – the Rescue of Stuart Diver*, which won a Gold Plaque at the Chicago International Television Festival and the highly successful min-series *The Day of the Roses* about the Granville Train Disaster. He also wrote the multi-award winning ABC TV series, *The Damnation of Harvey McHugh*. For his work in television John Misto has won three Australian Film Institute Awards, three Writers' Guild Awards and a Penguin Award.

John Misto also wrote a six part drama series, *The Cut* for ABC TV and a novel, *The Devil's Companions*, which was published in 2005.

Misto's latest play, *Dark Voyager*, premiers at Sydney's Ensemble Theatre in July, 2014.

Before becoming a writer, Misto studied Arts and Law at the University of New South Wales.

For the women who were there...

The Shoe-Horn Sonata

John Misto

Currency Press • Sydney

CURRENCY PLAYS

First published in 1996
by Currency Press Pty Ltd
Gadigal Land, PO Box 2287, Strawberry Hills, NSW, 2012, Australia
enquiries@currency.com.au
www.currency.com.au

Reprinted 1999, 2000 (twice), 2001, 2002, 2004, 2005, 2006, 2007, 2008, 2009, 2010, 2011, 2012, 2013, 2014, 2015, 2017, 2018, 2020, 2021, 2023.

NATIONAL LIBRARY OF AUSTRALIA CIP DATA

Misto, John, 1952–
    The shoe-horn sonata
    ISBN 9780868194813
    1. Women—Australia—Drama. 2. Ex-prisoners of war—Australia—Drama.
    I. Title.
A822.3

Cover design by Trevor Hood/Anaconda Graphic Design.

Front Cover: *Background* – Nurses from the Australian Army Nursing Service arrive at Singapore airfield, September 1945 for repatriation after three and a half years as prisoners of war of the Japanese in Sumatra. (Australian War Memorial negative number 044480); *Foreground* – Maggie Kirkpatrick as Bridie and Melissa Jaffer as Sheila in the Ensemble Theatre production, August 1995. (Photo: Michael Amendolia.)

All the production photos that appear within the text are of the August 1995 Ensemble Theatre production and were taken by Michael Amendolia.

Currency Press acknowledges the Traditional Owners of the Country on which we live and work. We pay our respects to all Aboriginal and Torres Strait Islander Elders, past and present.

Contents

Tangong, Singapore, 20 January 1942. Sisters of the Australian Army Nursing Service (AANS), 2/4th Casualty Clearing Station, 8th Division.

LEFT TO RIGHT:

(Back Row): *E. Millie Dorsch (VIC), drowned 14 February 1942; B. Peggy Willmott (WA), shot Banka Island Beach 15 February 1942; Wilhelmina R. Raymont (SA), died Banka Island February 1945; Elaine Balfour–Ogilvy, shot Banka Island Beach 15 February 1942; Peggy Farmaner, shot Banka Island Beach 15 February 1942.*

(Front row): *Dora S. Gardam (TAS), died Banka Island April 1945; Irene M. Drummond, later Matron of 2/13th Australian General Hospital, shot Banka Island Beach 15 February 1942 and Elaine M. Hannah who survived. Four of these nurses were among the twenty one army nurses massacred by the Japanese on Banka Island after the* SS Vyner Brooke *sank off Sumatra. The photographer, Warrant Officer J. D. Emmett became a prisoner of war after the surrender at Singapore and buried the film for nine months. It was then handed to a Private Abbott who developed it in the X-Ray Room at the Changi Hospital. After the war Warrant Officer Emmett recovered the film and had it printed. (Australian War Memorial Neg. No. A120518)*

The Unacknowledged

John Misto's *The Shoe-Horn Sonata* was first seen by audiences in 1995 during the year of *Australia Remembers*. The year when we remembered and thanked a generation who secured our freedom through the dark days of the Second World War. The play won the *Australia Remembers* National Playwriting Competition with a prize of $20,000. As a young teenager, John Misto read *White Coolies* written by Betty Jeffrey, a member of the Australian Army Nursing Service who, with twenty-three of her colleagues, survived captivity in Sumatra and Malaya. The story obsessed him for a number of years until he finally wrote this play.

The play centres on two characters—one a down to earth Australian Army Nurse with a Catholic background and the other, a young civilian English girl who meet after their ships have been sunk while fleeing from Singapore in 1942. They form a friendship which survives three and a half years of captivity as Prisoners of the Japanese Emperor in Camps in Malaya and Sumatra. Fifty years later, with other former prisoners, they meet at a reunion organised by a documentary maker. Neither is sure where this friendship is at, as no contact was made during the post war years. They are wary of each other and of renewing their friendship.

The shoe-horn was given to the Army Nurse by her father, a former World War One soldier when the nurse joins the Army. This item becomes useful in the camps, ultimately used as a metronome by the Choral Society which was formed by the prisoners. This society survives until illness and death deprives it of its members. Undeterred, the two friends form a Sonata as they live day by day under the brutality of their captors. While food and medicine become almost non-existent, they find their music cannot be taken from them and for a time it releases them from captivity and sets them free. As the story unfolds, we become aware that one has paid a terrible price to save her friend who is unaware of this sacrifice.

In the dark days during the fall of Singapore, sixty-five members of the Australian Army Nursing Service sailed under protest aboard the *Vyner Brooke* on 12 February 1942. Two days later this ship received several direct hits by Japanese aircraft and sank within half an hour. Twelve nurses were either killed or drowned in the water, others who swam or were in lifeboats made it to shore on Banka Island, Sumatra. One group of twenty-two nurses reached Radji beach together with some male survivors. After a time they gave themselves up to the Japanese who separated the men, marched them behind a bluff and on their return began cleaning their bayonets.

They then ordered the nurses to march into the sea and shot them in the back. One nurse survived, Vivien Bullwinkle, who managed to feign death and eventually escaped into the jungle where she met a male survivor. Together they survived in the jungle for several days eventually deciding to give themselves up to the Japanese.

The surviving thirty-two nurses were reunited after several days and spent the next three and a half years together with civilian women and children and British Army Nurses in camps throughout Sumatra and Malaya. The nurses were to lose another eight of their number before being repatriated and returning to Australia at the end of the war.

During their captivity they were deprived of food, medicine, often humiliated and beaten by their captors. Of the original sixty-five only twenty-four survived. Today those still alive remain a tightly knit group revered by soldiers, in particular those men of the 8th Division who themselves suffered under Japanese hands.

This play highlights a part of Australian military history that is not well known. Australian Army Nurses were Prisoners of War along with soldiers, sailors and airmen and suffered as did their male colleagues. All were deprived of basic comforts and the freedom which we take so much for granted in today's society. Some members of the audience were no doubt surprised to find this play was inspired by actual events.

The playwright donated his $20,000 prize to the Royal College of Nursing, Australia, which has formed the Nurses' National Memorial Committee. This committee is working towards creating a Memorial to Military Nurses, who have 'served, suffered and died in the cause of humanity', on Anzac Parade, Canberra. This gesture has been

Singapore, September 1945. Nurses from 2/10th and 2/13th Australian General Hospital and one survivor (Sister Mavis Hannah) from the 4th Casualty Clearing Station, aboard the Vyner Brooke *when it sank. After three and a half years as prisoners of war of the Japanese they have arrived at the airfield by RAAF plane from Sumatra for repatriation. They wear their original uniforms, incomplete and oil-stained. (Australian War Memorial Neg. No. A44480)*

greatly appreciated by all members of the nursing profession and former military nurses and stands as an inspiration in the fight towards recognition.

Jan McCarthy is a former Director, Nursing Services Army 1988–1992, Member of the Nurses' National Memorial Committee and currently Honorary Colonel and Representative Honorary Colonel, Royal Australian Army Nursing Corps.

Scores to be Settled

John Misto's play *The Shoe-Horn Sonata* is as much the untold story of hundreds of thousands of women imprisoned by the Japanese in South East Asia as a ringing indictment against Australian indifference to the lot of these women. The internees, who included Australian Army nurses, are the forgotten war trauma victims who were just left 'to get on with life'. Well known are the tales about the Burma Railroad, the POWs of Changi, Sandakan and other places, but who has ever heard of Muntok, Belalau ('the camp nobody talks about'), Cideng, Adek or Tangerang? If the play goes beyond the familiar and comfortable, it is precisely the playwright's intention to startle his audience with unquestionable facts. This is no fiction. It is a slice of potent historical evidence!

In October 1994 I received a letter from John Misto, requesting an interview to enable him to write the play 'as honestly and accurately as possible'. I readily acceded. Having been a teenage prisoner of the Japanese during the Great War, I had begun a campaign a few years earlier, through letters to the major newspapers, to try and redirect the public outpourings of sympathy for the victims of Hiroshima by pointing out that there exists a large group of victims of the Japanese, who for years mouldered and died in prisons rife with disease and vermin. These women and children were not annihilated in one superblast, but went through years of hell. They were innocent, many of them were Australians, and they still continue to suffer.

The interview with John Misto, who traced me through one of my letters, left me quite elated. Here, at last, was someone who had recognised the injustice, and who was not only prepared to, but eminently capable of, addressing the imbalance in public perception. During our talks I learnt that successive Australian governments had ignored the right of female ex prisoners for recognition and compassion. As Bridie remarks in the play: 'They told us we were on our own, just as they told us to keep smiling.' (Referring to a message 'to keep smiling' from Prime Minister Curtin, conveyed by the Japanese guard to the starving, dying Army nurses).

John Misto proved to be an exceptionally sensitive, perceptive and discreet interviewer, whose questions showed a deep knowledge of his subject, the result of intensive research. They were directed less at my personal experiences than at how—without the benefit of modern de traumatisation procedures—I 'got on with life'. After some groping (I'd never thought about it), I found the answer in the words of the character Sheila in the play, 'When something hurts you run away… Or you dig a hole and bury it.' Most survivors of trauma do both; they don't want to talk about it and sweep unwelcome memories into some vast garbage bag below the level of consciousness. Sooner or later the repressed memories start to fester, translating themselves into physical pain which cannot be ignored without fatal consequences. You either haul them out and tell, or die slowly. Such unassisted cases of self rehabilitation can take between thirty and fifty years, hence the recent spate of war stories from those who can finally tell.

In *The Shoe-Horn Sonata* (an aptly chosen title) the craft of the skilful playwright is demonstrated by the choice of a simple implement—a shoe horn—to centre the plot. It unites both narrative and dialogue, and acts as catalyst for dramatic revelations. To one party the shoe horn is a good luck omen; to the other a symbol of fear, pain and degradation; to both—eventually—the means of reconciliation, when the shoe horn is restored to its owner—'The war is over for us'. It plays a role in the prisoners' survival: 'Fifty voices and a shoe horn set us free.' It is indispensable for burying the dead, when a spade is the stuff of dreams along with juicy steaks, fresh fruit and soap.

There is pathos, friction, role reversal and anguished introspection moving the two women. Who saved whose life? Who was whose keeper? The impartial interviewer (a disembodied voice) brings about a re-examination of values and truths fifty years on, leading to devastating insights. Would Bridie have saved Sheila's life by selling her body for quinine? Rather than answering the question the other is reproached for not letting her die. But in the antiseptic world of the nursing sister such sacrifice is both repugnant and of an enormity beyond match.

The creative use of humour brings a freshness to the play which enables interest to be sustained; unrelieved misery would have created a feeling of depression. Humour defuses situations verging on the maudlin; it softens too abrasive exchange; it highlights the comic aspects of painful incidents. Setting the play in the present time, and working through the women's collective memories, was a brilliant idea. It is possible to laugh today at what was far from a laughing matter at the time it happened. Light banter is quite inconsistent with life and death situations, when even a smile would have set off the wrath of some Japanese guard.

Especially poignant is the women's shared reminiscence of their harrowing climb, whipped on by the enemy, to the top of a hill, where they expect to be executed. It is a fitting apotheosis of their endurance, their suffering and their final reconciliation. Fifty years of unexpressed grief, undeclared affection and unrevealed secrets are dissolved in their re-affirmation of a comradeship that has withstood time and the most lacerating of circumstances. This scene leaves very few dry eyes amongst the audience.

The Shoe-Horn Sonata opened at the Ensemble Theatre, Sydney, on 3 August 1995. I was privileged to be one of the invitees and—as John Misto put it—one of his most important critics. For me it was an overwhelming, even a cathartic, experience. It is not easy to live through those times again, to be transported through the agonies of starvation, deprivation of freedom, beatings and long stretches of dull despair, to experience again the undiluted terror of being delivered to a totally ruthless, brutish and brutal enemy with no protection from law or authorities. This is a fear that is inexpressible, incomprehensible to those who have never experienced it, a dread that strikes at the root of one's survival—an existential fear. It is what Bridie experiences when she is surrounded by Japanese tourists and flees from the store in utter panic.

The Shoe-Horn Sonata has to be classed as a first in calling public attention to the atrocities suffered by women at the hands of the Japanese. The voice of women is not heard often enough in a male dominated society in general, and in professions such as the military, in particular. John Misto has whipped aside the curtain and revealed the unsuspected, little known and sheer unbelievable acts of sadism and depravity committed against women in captivity. Far from making concessions because of gender, the Japanese treated women often more brutally even than men. This is not surprising when one reflects that in their hierarchically structured society women are at the bottom of the heap—just objects to be used at will.

The campaign for justice and compensation still goes on. The former Army nurses are still without a fitting memorial to their service during the war, their heroism and endurance during captivity. So far, Australian governments have shown little inclination to give them and other ex internees full recognition. Japanese governments have let their 'war heroes' get away with much more than simple murder. Instead of bringing them to justice as war criminals, they are being paid regular homage at their sacred shrine in Tokyo.

Today, more than fifty years after the end of World War II we have a situation where scores still remain to be settled. John Misto has brought this to our attention most dramatically.

July 1996

Vera Harms was imprisoned by the Japanese as young girl in Indonesia. She endured three years' captivity in several Japanese concentration camps.

Further Reading

The Forgotten Ones, Shirley Fenton-Huie, Angus & Robertson, Sydney, 1992.

You Can't Eat Grass, Eve ten Brummelaar, Image Desktop Publishing, 1996.

White Coolies, Betty Jeffrey, Angus & Robertson, Sydney, 1954.

In Japanese Hands, Jessie Elizabeth Simons, William Heinemann, Melbourne, 1954.

Captives, Catherine Kenny, University of Queensland Press, Brisbane, 1986.

Women Beyond the Wire, Lavinia Warner & John Sandilands, Michael Joseph, London, 1982.

The Fall of Singapore, Timothy Hall, Methuen, London, 1983.

Author's Note

Most teenagers do not expect to wake up and find themselves in a concentration camp. But this is exactly what happened to one hundred thousand school children in Asia and South East Asia in 1942. Overnight their countries were invaded and they were thrown without warning into Japanese prison camps.

When I was writing this play I spoke with many women who had been imprisoned in this way. In quiet Sydney homes on sunny afternoons, they poured tea and told me about bombings, shipwreck, massacres, torture, starvation, diseases and digging graves. They talked simply and calmly and without hate. There are several thousand of these women still living in Australia.

I would like to thank the following ladies for so generously sharing their wartime memories with me: Mrs Vera Harms, Mrs Pat Darling, Miss Patricia Kennedy, Mrs Pamela de Neumann, Mrs Catherine Spink, Mrs Elly Van Schie and Mrs Eve ten Brummelaar. I would also like to thank my friend and dramaturg, Heather Stewart, for her talent, faith and kindness.

When people ask why I wrote the play, this is what I tell them: In 1995 the United Nations announced that more civilians now die in war than soldiers. Yet they have no equivalent of Anzac Day on which their suffering is recognised. They are simply forgotten.

There is no national memorial to the many Australian nurses who perished in the war. At the time this play was first performed, the government had rejected all requests for one in Canberra.

I do not have the power to build a memorial. So I wrote a play instead. Although the characters of Bridie and Sheila are fictional, every incident they describe is true and occurred between 1942 and 1995.

There was even a shoe-horn…

The Shoe-Horn Sonata was first performed at the Ensemble Theatre on 3 August 1995, with the following cast:

BRIDIE	Maggie Kirkpatrick
SHEILA	Melissa Jaffer
VOICE OF RICK	Drayton Morley

Directed by Crispin Taylor
Sound design by Sarah De Jong
Lighting design by Alex Holver
Dramaturgy by Heather Stewart

CHARACTERS

BRIDIE
SHEILA

SETTING

A television studio; a motel room in Melbourne.

ACT ONE

Darkness. Out of the silence comes the voice of BRIDIE.

BRIDIE: [*raising her hands, clapping them twice sternly*] When the guard cries out 'Keirei!'—the female stands at complete attention, then bends her upper-body—so.

> BRIDIE *stands in a spotlight. She bows stiffly from the waist, and remains in this position.*

This kowtow is a tribute to the Emperor of Japan. Any bow that's less than perfect is a blasphemy against him... When the guard calls out 'Naore!'—the female straightens up again, without ever looking her master in the eye.

> BRIDIE *tries to straighten up, but her back is a little sore from this demonstration. An 'On-Air' sign becomes apparent.*

[*less formally*] They'd make us stand like that for hours—in the afternoon sun—in the middle of the jungle. I'd stare at the dirt and ask myself why I'd ever left Chatswood in the first place.

M. VOICE: And why did you?

BRIDIE: I guess I... wanted to be like my Dad. He'd been a soldier. Fought in Egypt. He didn't want me to enlist but I could tell that he was proud. The day I left for overseas, he gave me a present— [*Pulling a face*]— a shoe-horn of all things! He cleared his throat, looked downwards and said— [BRIDIE *puts her hands behind her back, and looks at the ground.*] 'There are three things every young soldier should know. Always use a shoe-horn [*Holding up an imaginary shoe-horn*]— it'll make your boots last longer. Don't sit on a toilet till you've lined the seat with paper. [*Awkwardly and rapidly*] And never kiss a Pommie on the lips.' [*Fondly*] Mum said he cried when my ship sailed off... I'd never been out of Australia before. I'd never been further than Woy Woy. But I didn't have time

1

to be homesick. As soon as we arrived we set up an army hospital—
just north of Singapore. Johore Bahru—it wasn't like Sydney—
that's for sure. There were chooks on the footpath—monkeys in
the trees—and the smell of fish-oil everywhere. Sometimes we'd
go dancing—all us nurses. It was hard to believe we were on the
brink of war.

> *Sound: 'Fall in Brother'—a popular marching song of the period.
> On the screen behind* BRIDIE *are projected several 1940 posters
> for the Women's Army. These are followed by photographs of the
> Australian army nurses disembarking in Singapore. They look
> excited and quite happy.*

> BRIDIE *sits in front of the screen. We realise she is sitting in
> a television studio where she is being interviewed for a
> documentary. There is a small table, with water, beside her.*

BRIDIE: I remember I asked an Englishman once—a captain with a
huge moustache—how dangerous the Japanese really were. 'My
dear,' he said. 'They have slanty eyes. If they can't see properly,
how can they shoot?' No one ever thought the Japs would get
within coo-ee of us. So the English didn't bother to fortify the
shore-lines. They said barbed wire would only spoil their beaches.
They dispensed with blackouts too. All of Singapore's lights were
fully ablaze when the Japanese bombers came. For a race that was
myopic, their aim was surprisingly accurate. I can still see those
Zeros flying over, hundreds of them—in V formations—their
engines rattling our hospital windows. We ran out onto the lawn
and watched. And I said to someone—a soldier I'd been nursing—
'I'm sure our planes will be waiting to greet them.' He looked at
me sadly—and smiled. 'But sister, don't you know? We don't have
a proper air-force. If the Japs can take Malaya, we'll be caught like
rats in a trap.' For the first time in months I started to long for quiet
little Chatswood…

M. VOICE: How did the English react to the bombing?

BRIDIE: Like a personal insult. 'Drive those little blighters out!' the
Governor told his troops. And off they went to do so… But we were
the ones who were driven out. Right out of Malaya. In a couple
of weeks. The whole of our army was forced back to Singapore—

where the Japs were bombing us day and night. Soon the hospitals were overflowing—there were wounded people everywhere—the halls, the stairs—even outside on the lawns. We all wore helmets—nurses and patients. And if a soldier didn't have one, we made him wear a bedpan. Towards the end—as the Japs got closer—some British officers held a meeting—to discuss the merits of shooting us. They promised we'd be buried with full military honours.

M. VOICE: You're not serious?

BRIDIE: Oh yes. They'd heard that the Japs had been raping army nurses and they thought they'd be doing us a favour. They're very considerate like that—the British. But since bullets were scarce, they decided to evacuate us. We didn't want to leave our patients. But we had no choice. I said goodbye to every one of them. Then we left on a ferry—the *Vyner Brooke*. It was built to carry 12. But it sailed that day with 300 people. We stood on deck—sixty-five army nurses—and watched the city burn. [*Sadly*] Singapore, Fortress of the Empire…

M. VOICE: Wasn't that a bit unsafe—cramming so many people onto a ferry?

BRIDIE: Some of the other ships were even more crowded.

M. VOICE: Other ships?

BRIDIE: There were forty-four all up.

M. VOICE: Forty-four ships times three hundred people— [*Surprised*] there were thirteen thousand of you?

BRIDIE: Probably more. The British had refused to evacuate civilians. They just couldn't believe that the Far East would fall. So they waited till the last—till the Japs had landed in Singapore. Then they threw their wives and children onto anything that would float… Just after we'd sailed the coastguard sent a telegram—warning the Navy to bring us all back. By the time someone decoded it, it was much too late for that. We were out in the middle of the South China Sea—thirteen thousand women and children—singing songs to pass the time. Well we mightn't have sung so loudly if we'd known about that telegram. What it said was very simple: some Japanese destroyers had been sighted in the area. [*Calmly*] And our forty-four ships were heading straight for them. [*Very calmly*] It was the thirteenth of February. Friday the thirteenth.

Darkness. Sound: very stirring chorus of 'Rule Britannia'— 'Britons never never never will be slaves'. Simultaneous projection of photographs of Singapore in 1942. They show a city at the height of its prosperity—and on the brink of a terrible catastrophe. We see its beautiful harbour; Raffles Hotel—the heart of the Empire; British matrons being waited on by Chinese servants—all the trappings of wealth and imperialism. Finally, as 'Rule Britannia' reaches its climax, we see a sign from 1941— put up by the government in Singapore. It says: 'Don't Listen to Rumour'.

If only they had...

SCENE TWO

Gradual lighting fades up to reveal a suggestion of a motel room— with a bar fridge. BRIDIE *and* SHEILA *enter and stop in the doorway. They are lugging two suitcases. There is a slight but obvious tension between them.* SHEILA *is carrying a pair of gloves.*

BRIDIE: [*with effort*] This is you. Just here.

> *They remain in the doorway.*

SHEILA: [*looking at suitcase*] We should have left these for the porter.

BRIDIE: [*disapprovingly*] And waste ten cents on a tip? We've carted bigger loads than this.

SHEILA: [*protesting*] We were fifty years younger then.

BRIDIE: Hah. It's all in the mind— [*Pulling back the curtain from the window*] Look at this—mountains—city—water. Best view in Melbourne.

SHEILA: [*concerned*] And the most expensive.

BRIDIE: [*slightly surprised*] Didn't they tell you? Everything's paid for. Just don't steal the towels.

SHEILA: Oh Bridie!

> BRIDIE *explores the bar area while* SHEILA *starts to unpack the smaller suitcase.*

SHEILA: So when do I start?

BRIDIE: First thing after lunch.

SHEILA: [*slightly dismayed*] So soon?

BRIDIE: It's just an interview. Not open-heart surgery.

SHEILA: But I've never been on TV before.

BRIDIE: You'll look ten kilos larger and slightly retarded. Rick says everyone does.

SHEILA: Rick?

BRIDIE: The interviewer... [*Fondly*] Gee it's good to see you.

> SHEILA, *who has been unpacking, appears to ignore this remark.*

SHEILA: [*concerned*] He's not like Donahue, is he? Strutting around like a turkey on heat—

BRIDIE: [*peeved, muttering*] And it's great to see you too, Bridie!

SHEILA: [*looking at* BRIDIE] You say something then? You'll have to talk into the good ear.

BRIDIE: Good ear? [*Notices the hearing aid and says quite loudly.*] How's that?

SHEILA: No need to shout...

BRIDIE: You'd better tell Rick you have a slight hearing problem.

SHEILA: Why?

BRIDIE: For when he asks questions.

SHEILA: [*with some concern*] What sort of questions is he asking?

BRIDIE: He just wants to hear some stories from the camp. [*Knowing what* SHEILA *is alluding to.*] Don't worry. He's very tactful.

SHEILA: He'd better be. If he's not I'll be turning this off. [*Indicating her hearing aid*]

BRIDIE: [*looking at* SHEILA *fondly as she unpacks*] Did you recognise me—just now—in the foyer?

SHEILA: Who could ever forget that big walk of yours?

BRIDIE: There was no mistaking you. No one else would carry gloves these days.

SHEILA: [*ironic smile*] It's the sign of a lady. Mother always used to say that. She wore her best pair into Changi. [*Noticing* BRIDIE'*s hand, with a hint of surprise*] Gosh—that's a wedding ring!

BRIDIE: [*smugly to* SHEILA] Who always used to say I'd end up an old maid?

SHEILA: Show me.

BRIDIE: [*letting* SHEILA *take her hand and look*] Dear Barnie. He's been gone for fifteen years now but I still miss him.

SHEILA: Children?

BRIDIE: Couldn't. [*Teasing*] I suppose you've had a dozen.

SHEILA: No. Never got round to marrying actually.

>   BRIDIE *looks up from the bar fridge, clearly astonished.*

[*indicating cashews* BRIDIE *is eating*] I hope that Rick is paying for those. They're $3.50 a packet… [*She continues unpacking*] Did many of the others come?

BRIDIE: Myra. Joyce. And Irene.

SHEILA: What about Ivy?

BRIDIE: Dead for years.

SHEILA: I'll always remember that voice of hers. [*Mimics*] 'They can starve me till my bones poke out—'

BRIDIE: [*joining in*] 'But I'll die without a fag, love.' Now that's a good story for Rick. Ivy and her smokes—those dried banana leaves she puffed on—God they had a terrible stink.

SHEILA: She pulled pages of her Bible out for cigarette papers. When it was over I heard her telling a minister that she'd survived the war because of the Good Book.

BRIDIE: Myra hasn't changed a bit. She still loves to gamble. She bet me five dollars you wouldn't show up.

SHEILA: Really?

BRIDIE: She was sure you'd consider it—'unrefined'—going on television—airing your feelings.

SHEILA: [*starting to unpack*] Well you've got to admit it's not very 'dignified'.

BRIDIE: So why did you come? [*Casually, trying to make light of it*] And don't say you did it for the chance of seeing me. Not after fifty years of hiding—

SHEILA: I wasn't hiding.

BRIDIE: You told me in 1945 you were going home to England. And I find out all this time you've been lying low in Perth.

SHEILA: Fremantle.

BRIDIE: [*almost casually—but not quite*] You could have written, Sheila. I presume there's a post office over there where they sell those little bits of paper we call stamps?

SHEILA *looks at* BRIDIE *with surprising intensity—but not with affection.* BRIDIE *looks back at* SHEILA, *desperately wanting her to say that she did come to see* BRIDIE. *A few seconds of silence. It is clear that something is still going on between these two women—even after fifty years' separation.* SHEILA *quickly turns to lift her suitcase onto the bed.*

BRIDIE: [*tersely*] You'll wreck your spine.

SHEILA: [*annoyed*] I know how to lift a suitcase thank you.

BRIDIE: [*taking charge—as usual*] We'll do it like we used to— [*Muttering, thinking she won't be heard*] if you can remember back that far?

SHEILA: That's the good ear, Bridie. [*Feeling she is being challenged*] And there's nothing wrong with my memory.

BRIDIE: Let's see then—shall we? [*Reciting with some intensity*] 'All womens will lift on the count of three. If you drop this coffin—'

SHEILA *joins in.*

BRIDIE & SHEILA: 'No rice tonight!'

BRIDIE begins to count as she grabs one end of the suitcase.

BRIDIE: Ichi—

SHEILA: Ni—

BRIDIE: San—

At the last second SHEILA *rises to the challenge and grabs the case as well. And together they heave it onto the bed. As they do this, they look at each other confrontingly and emit the Japanese call of—*

BRIDIE & SHEILA: Ya-ta!!!

It sounds almost like a war cry. Blackout.

SCENE THREE

Soundtrack: Dinah Shore singing a wistfully sad song from 1940—'Something to Remember You By'. The 'On-Air' Sign lights up.

SHEILA: [*v/o, nervously*] Hello? Can you hear me?

Then we hear a hand touching a microphone—a loud, uncomfortable sound.

BRIDIE: [*v/o*] Don't fidget with it, girl.

SHEILA: [*v/o*] Don't call me 'girl'!

M. VOICE: How long have you known Bridie?

BRIDIE: You'll have to speak up. She's a little deaf.

SHEILA: [*to* BRIDIE] I can hear him perfectly. [*To* RICK] For fifty three years. We met the night our ships were sunk. In February, 1942.

M. VOICE: Don't you think that your parents should have got you out sooner. They must have known for weeks that the Japanese were coming.

SHEILA: I… suppose they couldn't believe it.

BRIDIE: [*not meaning to be rude*] The British were a bit thick sometimes.

SHEILA: [*slightly annoyed*] We were patriotic. We didn't want to leave. I remember mother saying, 'Sheila, you and I are English women. We do not run away from a few Orientals… '

M. VOICE: But you did in the end.

SHEILA: [*defensively*] We had no choice.

Slides are projected onto a screen at the rear of the stage—photographs of the evacuation of 13 February, 1942. Images of women and children boarding ships, clutching toys and waving goodbye. It is hard to believe from their happy smiles that they are soon to be the victims of history's worst—and least known—massacre.

They put me on a boat for Brisbane. Mother insisted on staying behind—

BRIDIE: To stop the Japs looting her silver.

M. VOICE: Were you worried?

SHEILA: Not at all. [*Smiles*] It was quite a big adventure for a fifteen-year-old school girl.

BRIDIE: Tell him what your mother said.

SHEILA: Bridie!

BRIDIE: If you don't, I will!

SHEILA: [*slightly embarrassed*] Before I left mother said to me, 'You'll be living with Colonials now, so set a good example. Always wear gloves—wherever you go. Don't socialise with Catholics—unless they're French or titled. And never kiss an Australian on the lips.'

This remark earns a grunt from BRIDIE.

I was on a small ship. It was called the *Giang Bee*. It sailed out of Singapore with three hundred people. We were told we'd be back in a couple of weeks—so it was rather fun really. Like a trip up river. We all slept on deck. Under the moon. I woke up suddenly—about 3 a.m. There were people running everywhere. I could see them quite clearly, the deck was so bright. But this wasn't moonlight. The Japanese had found our ship and fixed a searchlight on it— to pin us in position. The strong, hard beams hit us square in the face. We lay flat on the deck and covered our eyes. But our sailors were yelling—'Get up! Stand up! Let the Japanese see you're just women and children.'

SHEILA *stands, fixed by a very, very bright spotlight.*

SHEILA: So we all stood up for the Japanese. Some mothers clutched their children and cried. And we stared into the light. For a while nothing happened. Just the roar of the sea—and us, ghostly white on the deck. Then there were flashes—like sparks in the distance— and the sounds of crackers going off. Women were screaming and running about—and some lay groaning and being trod on. Then sailors were yelling 'Jump for it! Jump for it!' One of them asked if I knew how to swim. 'A bit,' I replied. So he picked me up and threw me over. Next thing I found myself splashing around. [*Calmly*] And then there was this deafening noise. The whole of the ship rose up from the water—then crashed on its side. It lay there like a wounded animal, spilling oil instead of blood. [*Calmly*] It took less than a minute for the *Giang Bee* to sink. I'm not quite sure what happened next. I grabbed some wood to buoy me up—I didn't have a life-belt. I remember these toys came drifting by— tiny boats that really sailed and dolls with eyes that opened and stared. I clung to the wood and called for my mother. [*Angry*] Why did she have to stay behind? Who cared if the Japs took her beastly silver? Whenever I could I yelled for help. But the night was so dark and... nobody came.

M. VOICE: You must have been scared.

SHEILA: [*defensively*] Not really.

BRIDIE: Of course you were. She was petrified.

M. VOICE: What were you feeling then?

Sound: the distant sound of lapping waves as SHEILA *continues to speak.*

SHEILA: Shock, I suppose... and slimy from the oil. Oh I might have been nervous at first—when I realised I was all alone. But after a while a chill set in. It made me numb. And I didn't care. That's how the sea does it—that's how you drown. You can't think of anything but cocoa and a fire. My arms were aching from clinging to the wood, and I knew I couldn't hang on much longer. I shut my eyes and sang a hymn... so that Jesus would take me straight to Heaven. Though I'd have gone to Hell happily—provided it was warm.

Sound: YOUNG SHEILA *whimpering a line or two from 'Jerusalem'—a very moving and stirring hymn about the greatness of England—God's chosen Empire.*

Y. SHEILA: [*v/o*] 'Bring me my bow of burning gold!/ Bring me my arrows of desire!'

OLDER SHEILA *joins in.*

Y. SHEILA & SHEILA: 'Bring me my spear! O clouds unfold! Bring me my chariot of fire.'

SHEILA: But I can't have sung loudly enough. No fiery chariot came down for me. [*Trying to smile*] It was Friday night and there I was—drenched, without gloves, and alone on the sea. One week before I had been a schoolgirl. And I wasn't allowed out on a Friday night—not even with a chaperon.

Slides of Singapore Harbour are projected onto the screen—filled with burning ships. Clouds of smoke every where...

BRIDIE: My ship sank as well. Some Japanese Zeros found us. They dropped twenty-eight bombs on the *Vyner Brooke*. And twenty-seven missed. The one that got us went clean down the funnel and blew the ship from beneath our feet. Then the Japs strafed the decks and shot up all the life boats. Every one was surprisingly calm—from sheer disbelief I suppose. We behaved more like we were hopping off a bus than fleeing from a sinking ship. But soon we discovered that it wasn't the Japs who posed the biggest danger. Before we'd sailed from Singapore, the navy had given us life-jackets. They weren't the standard issue, though. And nobody told us that they had to be tied in a different way to the normal ones. So when our ship was ablaze and sinking, some women started to leap from the deck. I was just about to do likewise when an Army sister grabbed me. She waved and yelled, 'Bridie, don't jump!' Then she pointed down at the sea. Those women who'd jumped were floating quite well—but all of them were dead. They were killed the second they hit the water... Their navy issue life jackets broke their necks... We had no choice but to shimmy down ropes. Like most beginners I went too fast and burned my fingers raw.

M. VOICE: What was going through your mind as you struggled in the sea?

BRIDIE: I was... trying not to panic. I didn't know how to swim because my Dad had never taught me. 'No need,' he'd said. 'There's a mole on your neck. That means you'll never drown.' As I swallowed half the South China Sea, I hoped to God that Dad was right. But it's just like Sheila says. Drowning simply wears you out. I tried to say a rosary but I must have dozed off. Then a splashing sound woke me. I was sure it was a shark—till this little voice called out—'Weather's turned a bit chilly for this time of year.'

SHEILA *laughs*.

BRIDIE: Then she added—so politely—'I don't believe we've been introduced.'

SHEILA: [*almost indignant*] You can't remember what I said!

BRIDIE: I told her who I was and—she was just a bit stand-offish.

SHEILA: Cartwright is an Irish name. Mother wouldn't have approved.

BRIDIE: 'Another stuck up Pom,' I thought. But I talked to her anyway.

SHEILA: She wouldn't stop talking.

BRIDIE: I didn't have a choice. Sheila wasn't in a life-jacket—(she was) just clinging to some wood. And my hands were skinned so badly I couldn't hold her up. If she fell asleep, she'd have slipped away and drowned. So I asked her questions. Quizzed her on everything. Fashion—food—film stars. She liked Frank Sinatra. I preferred Bing Crosby.

SHEILA *sneers*.

Well we had a few words about that. But after a while she nodded-off anyway.

M. VOICE: So how did you keep her awake?

SHEILA: She hit me. That's how.

BRIDIE: Just a gentle tap. With my shoe-horn. I still had it in my pocket.

SHEILA: Wham! Right here. [*Indicates nose*] Every time I closed my eyes—

BRIDIE: [*mimics hitting*] Tap—tap—tap—

SHEILA: [*harsher*] Whack—whack—whack.

BRIDIE: Well it woke you up. And you know what she said on the fifth or sixth go? 'Cut it out, you Catholic cow!'

SHEILA: [*shocked*] That isn't true!

BRIDIE: I was tempted to let her sink. But Christian Charity won the day. So I tapped her again— [*Grins*]— just a little bit harder. Dad's shoe-horn came in very handy. I lost it—later in the war—otherwise I'd show you the best way to do it. But after a while I was too tired to hit her—even for the pleasure of it. A wave came up—caught us both unaware. It picked Sheila up and carried her off.

> *Once again we hear the sound of lapping waves which continues during* BRIDIE'*s speech.*

BRIDIE: I called and called. There was no reply. And I knew the poor kid must have drowned. I was saying a prayer—for her departed soul—when I heard this raspy voice above the waves. I was sure I was going mad because it... [*Amazed*] sounded like 'Jerusalem'... And there Sheila was—still clutching her wood... I was so darn relieved I even joined in. My Dad would have killed me—behaving like a Protestant.

> *We hear* YOUNG BRIDIE *and* YOUNG SHEILA *singing a few (waterlogged) lines from 'Jerusalem'.* OLDER BRIDIE *and* OLDER SHEILA *join in, hesitantly.*

ALL: 'I will not cease from mental fight,/ Nor shall my sword sleep in my hand,/ Till we have built Jerusalem/ In England's green and pleasant land.'

M. VOICE: How long did it take till you were washed-up on shore?

BRIDIE: [*ominously*] We weren't washed-up. We got a lift—thanks to this one. [*Indicating* SHEILA]

SHEILA: Just after dawn—when my nose felt like Pinnochio's—a ship came out of nowhere.

BRIDIE: Before I could stop her, she was yelling out and waving, 'Yoo-hoo, chaps. I say, Yoo-hoo!' [*Calmly*] But by then I could see the ship's flag.

And now, on stage, we see a large Japanese flag, the blood-red rising sun, which is gradually and brilliantly illuminated as the scene continues.

M. VOICE: How did you feel—when you realised?

BRIDIE: Too tired to care. And they didn't seem to notice us—as though we were rubbish that had drifted their way. We must have looked like rubbish too, bobbing about and covered in oil. Then one of them pointed—and yelled to his mates. Soon there were dozens of them lining the deck. And we could see that they were laughing at us.

SHEILA instinctively reaches out to take BRIDIE's hand. They hold hands. And once again they both look very vulnerable. We hear Japanese voices on the soundtrack.

SHEILA: I wanted to cry. [*With resolution*] But I reminded myself I was a Woman of the Empire. And it just wasn't done to show fear to the natives. [*Wistful smile*] I could almost hear my mother saying: 'Chin up, gel! And where are your gloves?'

Gradual darkness. The final rousing chorus of 'Jerusalem'.

CHORUS: 'Bring me my bow of burning gold!/ Bring me my arrows of desire!/ Bring me my spear! O clouds, unfold!/ Bring me my chariot of fire!/ I will not cease from mental fight,/ Nor shall my sword sleep in my hand,/ Till we have built Jerusalem/ in England's green and pleasant land.'/

As the chorus is sung, the Japanese flag fades and we see photographs of the Japanese invasion of Singapore—Japanese soldiers riding bicycles, a sky filled with parachutes; Japanese battalions marching through the streets. As the song reaches its climax, we see hundreds of victorious Japanese soldiers, their arms raised in triumph, performing a Bonzai! salute.

It is a most disturbing sight. For this photo has captured the very moment when the British Empire teetered and fell...

SCENE FOUR

BRIDIE *and* SHEILA *have just returned from the TV Studio. As they talk,* BRIDIE *studies the breakfast menu—a long strip of cardboard that has been left to hang on the door handle.*

BRIDIE: Went rather well I thought.

SHEILA: [*in disbelief*] Rather well? I rambled on like a freight train. And you let me.

BRIDIE: Don't be silly.

SHEILA: I got a bit flustered. Those lights were so bright—and then this [*Indicates hearing-aid*] started picking up static. I'll be the laughing-stock of WA.

BRIDIE: [*calmly corrects her*] You mean 'Australia'. It's a national show. [*Looks at the menu, puzzled*] 'Compost of fruit'?

SHEILA: [*correcting her tersely*] 'Com-pote'. Get your eyes tested.

BRIDIE: At least I can hear.

> BRIDIE *begins to look closely at* SHEILA*'s face.*

SHEILA: [*uneasily*] What are you doing?

BRIDIE: [*calmly*] Looking for lice… In camp when you were in a mood there was always something biting you.

SHEILA: [*moodily*] I am not in a mood.

BRIDIE: [*muttering*] You'd go around snapping and snarling for days. I haven't missed that—let me tell you…

> BRIDIE *goes back to studying her breakfast menu. No, she does not study it. She ticks everything on offer.*

SHEILA: And there was no need to call the British 'thick'.

> BRIDIE *deliberately ignores* SHEILA*'s rising anger. Indeed, she holds up some little motel coffee sachets and looks at them.*

BRIDIE: I might ask the maid for a few more of these. They're ten cents each at Franklins.

SHEILA: [*more insistent*] Bridie? Did you hear me?

BRIDIE: Well what was I supposed to say? It was a stroke of naval genius—sailing us straight into the Japanese fleet?

SHEILA: [*sternly*] You're just like your former Prime Minister—any excuse to bash the Poms. Well at least he got his come-uppance.

Meanwhile BRIDIE *casually picks up a glass that is in a 'hygienic' paper-seal bag.* BRIDIE *removes the paper, holds the glass up to the light, shakes her head in dismay, and goes off to wash it. Her conversation with* SHEILA *continues.*

BRIDIE: That's a side of you I'd forgotten. Sheila the Patriot. [*Sarcastically*] It must have been hard to live out here—when your heart was so firmly entrenched in England. I take it you've actually been there.

SHEILA: [*firmly*] One never stops being British. Nor does one want to.

BRIDIE: [*sarcastically*] God forbid.

SHEILA: Perhaps Singapore wasn't our finest hour—

BRIDIE: [*with growing annoyance*] Not 'our finest hour'! My dear girl—

SHEILA: Stop calling me that. I'm not a child now.

BRIDIE: [*ignoring this rebuke*]… it was the biggest debacle since the Greeks took Troy. And I'll bet you at Troy there was some British general's forbear saying [*Mimics cruelly*] 'What a smashing wooden horse! I say chaps, wheel her in!'

SHEILA: You can snicker all you like— [*Struggling to explain*] but at the very worst times in the camp—I'd remind myself I was part of an Empire—and if others could endure it, so could I.

BRIDIE *snorts.*

SHEILA: [*defensively*] It got me through the war.

BRIDIE: I got you through the war. Your Empire didn't give a damn. They left you to the Japs.

SHEILA: [*very upset*] If you say that tomorrow, I'll go. I mean it. And I hope you choke on your compost of fruit.

BRIDIE: [*getting annoyed*] Well that leaves me in a nice little fix. If I criticise the English, you'll pack up and depart. If I get stuck into the Nips, I'll be branded a racist. So what do I talk about from 1942? The weather?

As SHEILA *is about to depart,* BRIDIE *calls her back.*

BRIDIE: [*with both fear and anger showing*] Don't you dare walk out on me again!

SHEILA *stops, turns, and looks at* BRIDIE.

BRIDIE: [*more placatory*] It's hard—I know—your first time on camera… At least have a nightcap before you go… We shouldn't be wasting our time together fighting. We never did in camp.

SHEILA: [*astounded*] We fought all the time. You were worse than my mother.

BRIDIE: I could hardly sit back and let you run wild. You had to have guidance—from someone mature.

SHEILA: Guidance? You mean a barrage of orders. [*Mimics her*] 'Sheila—did you eat your grass? [*Sternly*] Why haven't you drunk your charcoal water?' God how I hated that stuff.

BRIDIE: It helped you keep your food down. And got rid of all those stomach pains.

SHEILA: [*softening a little—and teasing also*] And as for 'mature'— [*Accusingly*]— Who wasn't sure what a loin-cloth was?

BRIDIE: Up till then I'd only seen boxer shorts.

SHEILA: You spent ages working out which bit went where—and how the Japanese tied them on.

BRIDIE: [*slightly defensive*] I had to know—to do the job. [*She stops, suddenly inspired*] I could talk about that tomorrow—about our favourite pastime in camp.

SHEILA: [*shocked but amused*] You wouldn't dare.

BRIDIE: [*as she pours the drinks*] I'll look calmly at the camera and say 'During the war we made loin-cloths for the Japs.'

SHEILA: [*to imaginary camera*] Bridie's knowledge of the male anatomy helped make them comfy for our lords and masters.

BRIDIE: [*to camera*] While Sheila used her needlework skills to sew little daisies around the edges.

[*pouring drinks*] And then—one wonderful morning—Lipstick Larry comes strutting out to *tenko*—wearing some of our handiwork beneath his baggy shorts…

SHEILA: Up goes the flag. He calls out Keirei! And everybody bows… including Lipstick Larry. [*To* BRIDIE] I'll never know how you managed to do it—stitch a rusty pin into his loin-cloth.

BRIDIE *and* SHEILA *bow together. On the soundtrack we hear* LIPSTICK LARRY *yelling from a stab of excruciating pain.* BRIDIE *and* SHEILA *laugh. Then the angry voice of* LIPSTICK LARRY *shouting abuse in Japanese. Then we hear* YOUNG BRIDIE'*s voice.*

Y. BRIDIE: [*v/o*] I'm sorry, sir. It's all my fault. I lost my glasses when the— [*ship went down*].

> *Another savage yell from* LIPSTICK LARRY, *followed by the ugly thumps of* YOUNG BRIDIE *being punched and hit. We hear a very* YOUNG SHEILA.

Y. SHEILA: [*v/o*] Bridie! Bridie!

Y. BRIDIE: [*v/o, very calmly*] It's all right, dear. Get back in line.

> *As* BRIDIE *and* SHEILA *remember this, they cease laughing. Their attitude is now one of 'At least we got that bastard.'*

SHEILA: The look on his face—God that was funny!

BRIDIE: Best moment of the war! [*Raising her glass*] To needlework.

SHEILA: And rusty pins.

BRIDIE & SHEILA: [*amicably as they clink glasses*] Ya-ta!!

> *Then* BRIDIE *and* SHEILA *drink. On the soundtrack we can still hear* LIPSTICK LARRY *beating* BRIDIE. *Blackout.*

SCENE FIVE

Sound: 'Happy Times' by Jo Stafford as the 'On Air' sign lights up. BRIDIE *and* SHEILA *are sitting side by side, being interviewed.* BRIDIE *hesitates and looks at* SHEILA.

BRIDIE: [*calmly*] Twelve nurses didn't make it when the *Vyner Brooke* went down. They died from drowning or… sharks or… their life jackets. Twenty-two others struggled to shore —at Radji Beach on Banka Island. They were looking after wounded sailors when the Japanese found them. All the men were bayoneted. Then the Japs forced the nurses to march into the sea. One of the nurses said to her friend—'Two things I hate most in this world are Japs and water. Now I've got them both. Well it couldn't get worse.'

> *The sounds of machine gun fire—and the cries of women—on the soundtrack.*

BRIDIE: There was one survivor, Vivien Bullwinkel… My friends weren't a threat—they were only there to help people. I'll never understand why the Japs had to shoot them.

We see photographs of the women in Japanese prison camps— lining up for food, sleeping in barracks, carrying water. These photos are shown as SHEILA *and* BRIDIE *continue to speak.*

SHEILA: Our Japs picked us up and took us to Sumatra. That's Indonesia now.

BRIDIE: [*still upset*] He knows where it is.

SHEILA: We were taken to a camp. It was really a few suburban streets hemmed in by barbed wire. Eight hundred of us—women and children packed into fourteen bungalows. There were nuns as well. And missionaries. I lived in a garage—with Bridie and the army nurses.

BRIDIE: She kicked up a fuss, believe me. Said she wanted to 'flat' with some school chums. That's when I put my foot down. A child like her—unsupervised—with Japanese all around. She fought at first but she soon learned who was in charge.

M. VOICE: Was this camp like a normal gaol?

BRIDIE: [*tersely*] I've never been in a normal gaol.

SHEILA: If you're sent to a gaol you know why you're there. But we hadn't broken any law.

BRIDIE: And most prisoners are told how long they'll be in for. We didn't have a clue. Months. Years. It was anyone's guess. Not knowing was the worst part.

SHEILA: No—the toilets were the worst part. Filthy pits—dug out in the open. We weren't allowed privacy.

BRIDIE: You had to squat—in front of everyone—even the guards. And they'd always watch. They wanted to humiliate us.

SHEILA: I told myself I'd rather burst—then I'd try and hold off till dark… but there was always a Jap standing by the latrine.

BRIDIE: No toilet paper either.

M. VOICE: So what did you use?

BRIDIE: Leaves. The trees were stripped in a couple of weeks… And I don't mind saying that it got a bit awkward when a certain time of the month came round…

SHEILA: [*horrified, hissing*] Bridie!

BRIDIE: [*defensively to* SHEILA] Well it happened… But after a while we stopped. Thank goodness.

M. VOICE: [*surprised*] You stopped menstruating? All of you?

SHEILA: Just the women.

BRIDIE: We didn't start again till the war was over… It was fear that did it. Fear and rotten food.

SHEILA: Those first few weeks were a nightmare. Women sobbing for their husbands. Babies crying—always hungry. And the Japs'd come round and beat us for the fun of it. 'Useless Mouths' they used to call us.

> On the screen we see a photograph—the face of a Japanese soldier, very much a warrior, fierce and terrifying. A few seconds' silence, then…

M. VOICE: Did the Japanese ever try to take advantage of you?

SHEILA: Not really.

M. VOICE: In the whole of the war they never came near you? That's hard to believe after what you've been saying.

> SHEILA and BRIDIE look at each other awkwardly.

BRIDIE: [uneasily] Oh they tried it once. The Japs had a house—an 'officers' club'. We nicknamed it 'Lavender Street'—after the red-light district in Singapore. They ordered the Australian nurses to be 'hostesses' there.

SHEILA: They got the idea from a prisoner—an Australian—he set it up.

BRIDIE: [annoyed] We don't know for sure he did.

SHEILA: [to camera] People blame the British for Singapore. There were Aussies too who were hardly saints.

BRIDIE: [annoyed with SHEILA] Have you forgotten how many of the British collaborated? [To the camera] The Japs wanted us because they knew they couldn't have us. But they could pick and choose from amongst the Poms. Those women who'd lorded it over everyone at Raffles were selling themselves for a hard-boiled egg.

SHEILA: They had no choice. They had children to feed. We didn't judge. We accepted it.

BRIDIE: [disgusted] I didn't! To go with a Jap—to give him pleasure—how could you ever live with yourself?

M. VOICE: [diplomatically] Well let's try and get back to my original question. What exactly happened at Lavender Street?

BRIDIE: Twelve army nurses were ordered to attend the opening night of this… glorified brothel. We had no choice but to go. We spent hours getting ready—greasing our hair down—putting dirt under our nails. All of us were terrified—but we couldn't let it show. If the Japs smelled fear, you were finished. Some Japanese officers were waiting with saki. Saki and biscuits. Soon they were getting drunk and gropey—and in no time at all we were fending them off. We knew what they'd done to other nurses—raped them and killed them—in Hong Kong and Singapore. So we smiled. We bowed. Then shook our heads. The Japs were getting fed up with this. They told everyone to go. [*Ominously*] Except for four of the nurses.

M. VOICE: Were you one of them?

BRIDIE: [*reluctantly*] Yes… At the Chatswood dances I'd always been a wallflower. Now here was this Jap giving me the eye. He thrust a glass of saki at me. [*Bowing her head*] I said 'Thank you, sir. May you always have syphilis.' He didn't understand. In fact my resistance seemed to excite him. His cheeks were red and he was dribbling. I kept filling his glass with saki as I tried to wriggle away. My friends were doing much the same. Except for one. [*Slightly surprised*] She was laughing and… smiling and getting on really well with her Jap. [*Shocked*] I couldn't believe it. One of us giving in! But every time he'd go to kiss her, she'd giggle and flirt and… cough—very slightly. [*Very surprised*] And he'd suddenly pull away. She did this—oh—half a dozen times. Then finally—with great apology—she produced a small rag—to use as a hanky. It was spotted with blood. The Japanese weren't scared of much—but tuberculosis terrified them. And this lass knew it. She'd taken the rag from the hospital hut and used it as a last resort. That dirty rag saved all our lives. Soon I was coughing and so were the others. The Japs gave up and sent us home… That night turned me off blind dates forever.

Darkness. Then we see a photograph of children in a Japanese prison camp. They are stick-thin, obviously starving, dressed in rags, filthy.

SHEILA: Those first few months we were always hungry. It took our stomachs ages to shrink. So for morning tea we used to have this.

SHEILA *holds up a small chop bone.* BRIDIE *looks at it fondly.*

BRIDIE: [*mutters, amazed*] Oh, Lord… I don't believe it… Show me…

SHEILA, *smiling, passes the chop bone to* BRIDIE.

M. VOICE: What is that exactly?

BRIDIE: [*almost impatiently*] A chop-bone of course!

SHEILA: [*to* BRIDIE] I couldn't bring myself to throw it away.

BRIDIE *examines it.*

BRIDIE: [*fondly*] We'd chew on this every night before bed. We called it Old Reliable.

SHEILA: [*nostalgically*] And as we chewed, we'd talk about food.

BRIDIE: Hold imaginary dinner parties—

SHEILA: Swap recipes—

BRIDIE: Plan menus—

M. VOICE: [*amazed*] And you shared a bone—like… [*He's too tactful to say it.*]

SHEILA: [*calmly, without taking offence or seeing anything wrong the suggestion*] Dogs? Yes. We shared everything.

M. VOICE: [*puzzled and surprised*] Why didn't you just give up and— ?

BRIDIE: Die? Many women did… And quite a few went out of their minds—so the Japs took them off and killed them.

SHEILA: We were all a bit gloomy. It became quite a problem. Then some British women—these wonderful missionaries—decided to cheer us up.

'Bolero' is heard faintly in the background and continues for the rest of the scene.

They announced they were forming an orchestra—no mean feat since we didn't even have a tin drum in camp.

M. VOICE: Were they serious?

SHEILA: Oh yes. One of them had written a score—so that each woman's voice could sing the part of an instrument. Flutes. Violins. She even had trumpets. They asked me to audition—because I could read music.

BRIDIE: I went along to watch. I was quite green with envy. It looked like lots of fun. Well as I was standing there, this missionary came over. Her name was Miss Dryburgh. 'My dear,' she said, 'that thing around your neck—is that a shoe-horn?' I'd been wearing it, you see—so it wouldn't get lost—

SHEILA: Or stolen.

BRIDIE: Miss Dryburgh peered at it and said 'Perfect. Perfect. Just what we need.' 'But we don't have shoes,' I told her. 'No, my dear. But now we have a metronome.' So I, Bridie Cartwright, became part of a choir—without having to read a note of music. Oh we were just a bunch of amateurs in a prison camp in the corner of the jungle. But to us we became the Glen Miller Orchestra and the London Philharmonic all rolled into one. We held our first concert after eight weeks of practice.

SHEILA: We sang 'Bolero'. Ravel's 'Bolero'.

BRIDIE: I stood out front—like this [BRIDIE *stands*] tapping my shoe-horn to keep the pace while Miss Dryburgh conducted. [*Taps her imaginary shoe-horn.*]— andante—allegro—prestissimo!

SHEILA: Hundreds listened.

BRIDIE: Some even cried.

We hear 'Bolero' as BRIDIE *conducts.*

SHEILA: We forgot the Japs—we forgot our hunger—our boils—barbed-wire—everything… Together we made this glorious sound that rose above the camp—above the jungle—above the war—rose and rose and took us with it. Fifty voices set us free.

BRIDIE: Fifty voices and a shoe-horn…

More 'Bolero'. Stirring. Majestic and ultimately triumphant. Blackout.

SCENE SIX

SHEILA'*s hotel suite. The lights come up on an empty set.* BRIDIE *and* SHEILA *can be heard – then seen as they emerge from the bathroom or hall, in a two-person conga line, singing brightly and moving rhythmically to an old but popular song from their POW camp. The song is sung to the tune of Percy Grainger's 'English Country Gardens'.*

BRIDIE & SHEILA: [*singing*] 'How many kinds of food do we eat/ in our daily prison diet?/ Here is our main course, entree and sweet./ Keep your rumbling stomachs quiet./ Rice for breakfast./ Rice for lunch./ Rice for supper./ Rice for brunch./ Rice for tiffin./ Rice for tea./ Fry it. Boil it. Stew it. Poach it thrice./ Rice will always taste like—bloody rice!'

At the end of the song, BRIDIE *makes a flourishing gesture.*

SHEILA: We can't do this. We'll look ridiculous.

BRIDIE: [*firmly*] But I've promised the girls we'd join in.

SHEILA: [*almost accusingly*] I refuse to make a fool of myself for a few cheap laughs on Rick's show… I don't like him, Bridie. You should have warned me he'd be asking those questions.

BRIDIE: [*annoyed*] You didn't have to answer them… I don't know why you bothered to come. You've been sour as a pickle from the moment you arrived. And don't think your little dig went unnoticed.

SHEILA: What dig?

BRIDIE: About the Australian—who offered us to the Nips. It's not patriotic to attack our men.

SHEILA: So why did you mention the British women selling themselves for food? The way you put it—it sounded so—crass.

BRIDIE: It was crass, Sheila. [*Relents a little*] I didn't mean to tell him but he put me on the spot…

SHEILA: They were people I grew up with. A lot of them were friends of mine.

BRIDIE: And the Japs were the enemy. Every woman who gave in made it harder for the rest.

SHEILA: It was the only way they could feed their kids.

BRIDIE: [*with disgust*] Sleeping with a Jap? I'd never have done that—not for anyone. How could you go on living with yourself—or look your family in the eye?

> *This is a shattering remark for* SHEILA, *but she does her best to conceal any reaction.*

You agreed with me—if I remember. When Sylvia Green went off with a Nip, you said you'd have her barred from every bridge club in Malaya.

> BRIDIE *goes to the bar area, peers around it, and grabs some food. Then* BRIDIE *notices some snapshots of* YOUNG SHEILA *lying near the bar fridge.* BRIDIE *looks at them. They catch her off guard.* SHEILA *turns away, embarrassed, and busies herself with making tea or whatever.*

SHEILA: Rick asked to see photos—of things before the war.

> BRIDIE *looks at the photos, and smiles very sadly.*

BRIDIE: I'd know this creature anywhere… the stuck-up way she held her head… those ridiculous gloves… [*Disturbed*] Why didn't you get married?

> SHEILA, *who has not actually heard the question, turns.*

SHEILA: What?

BRIDIE: I said—can you give me a copy of this?

SHEILA: Why? I look awful.

BRIDIE: [*trying to sound casual about it*] I just like to have photos… of my friends.

SHEILA: [*not too callously*] People always get on when they're tossed in together. I'd hardly call that friendship.

BRIDIE: I brought something along to show you.

> *And* BRIDIE *produces a small tobacco tin.*

SHEILA: It's just an old tin.

BRIDIE: [*annoyed*] Your memory must have gone with your hearing. You gave this to me. For my birthday. In 1942.

> SHEILA *takes the tin and looks at it. It's obvious she remembers—
> but is concealing it.*

When I was sick from dengue fever. And because I couldn't work, the Japs refused to feed me. God I was hungry. I believe I cried. Then you appeared. You said: 'Happy birthday, Bridie!'—and you thrust this rusty tobacco tin at me [*Indicating the tin*]… and inside there was some rice that you'd fried up with banana skin… [*Still touched by the thought*] You gave me your dinner.

SHEILA: [*lying and pretending it was no big deal*] A few spoons of rice. I didn't even miss them.

BRIDIE: It was food. Your food. And you were starving. So we sat down and ate it together. It was the best birthday present anyone's ever given me… [*Looking at the photo with great tenderness and sadness*] I miss her sometimes—little Sheila. [*Looking tenderly at* SHEILA] I'd give anything to bring her back.

> BRIDIE *looks at* SHEILA *with sudden and desperate affection.*
> SHEILA *tries to resist the force of this emotion and turns away.*
> BRIDIE *feels embarrassed at showing* SHEILA *how much she still
> cares for her.*

BRIDIE: [*glancing at her watch*] 'Struth. We'd better get a move on—or we'll miss out on the entree. [*She hesitates*] I'm sorry if I said too much. To Rick I mean. I can be an old bore sometimes. [*Feeling hurt and hiding it*] See you downstairs in twenty minutes.

> SHEILA *nods.*

And don't tell the waiter that you never eat dessert. If you don't want your pavlova, I'll have it.

> BRIDIE *exits.* SHEILA *goes to a drawer, takes out a shoe-horn, and looks at it very sadly.*

> *In the background the distant sound of crickets—and we hear* YOUNG SHEILA.

Y. SHEILA: [*v/o frightened*] Please—please—don't send me away. I'll do whatever you want. I promise.

> *And then we hear some* MEN *speaking Japanese, and a* JAPANESE SOLDIER.

SOLDIER: [*v/o*] Name?

Y. SHEILA: [*v/o*] Sheila. My name is Sheila.

> *The* SOLDIER *translates the name into Japanese. Then we hear other* JAPANESE *soldiers laughing.*

SOLDIER: [*v/o*] You sing now, Sheila. Speedo! Speedo!

> YOUNG SHEILA *begins to sing. We can hear* JAPANESE SOLDIERS *laughing and clapping. But as the song progresses they are so moved by it that they grow silent.*

Y. SHEILA: [*v/o*] 'It's a… lovely day tomorrow… Tomorrow is a… lovely day… come and feast your tear-dimmed eyes… on tomorrow's clear blue skies… '

> SHEILA *stares sadly at the shoe-horn as she remembers.*

> *On the screen we see two photographs of women prisoners of the Japanese. They are in a shocking state, huddled on dirty, makeshift beds. These former rulers of the British Empire are now skin and bone and dressed in rags. They stare at the camera with despairing eyes.*

SCENE SEVEN

We see photos of some women POW's—emaciated, haggard, impoverished.

M. VOICE: Were you ever that bad?

> BRIDIE *stands in a spotlight.*

BRIDIE: [*calmly*] We were worse. The lightest I got was exactly five stone. And Sheila was a bit under four. I know I'm right because the Japs used to weigh us—every month—all the women in the camp. It was part of some experiment—to see how thin our bodies could get before we started dying. The Japs, as you know, wouldn't give us any medicine. Not even to the children. So we all made Wills... I can still remember mine. [*Recites*] 'In the event of my death, I, Brigid Mary Cartwright, bequeath all my possessions to my good friend Sheila Richards... These possessions being—my shoe-horn engraved with the letters BMC, my tobacco tin, and my half-share in our caramel.'

M. VOICE: [*amused*] Your caramel?

BRIDIE: Don't laugh. It was important. Caramel was our only luxury. Sheila sold her brooch to buy some—from a native who used to smuggle it. Every week—on Sunday night—we'd pop that caramel into our mouths—for one minute each—one minute of bliss—then we'd store it away till the next week.

M. VOICE: You were never tempted to eat it all?

BRIDIE: No. We were very strict about that. It had to last till the end of the war.

M. VOICE: And did it?

BRIDIE: Not quite. In 1943 our will-power crumbled. And we ate the lot.

M. VOICE: [*almost accusingly*] Why? What happened?

BRIDIE: [*embarrassed*] It's only caramel. You don't want to know.

M. VOICE: Of course I do. What happened?

BRIDIE: Christmas. That's what. [*Bleakly*] You don't know what Christmas is like in a camp. Hungry women—dirty rice. Rumbling stomachs instead of carols. And all you can think about is your family at home—a thousand miles away—sitting down to turkey and ham. I was picking weevils out of my food when out of the blue—I began to hear voices—

We hear singing on the soundtrack—distant at first but gradually getting louder. Twenty or thirty men joyfully singing 'O, Come All Ye Faithful'.

BRIDIE:— deep male voices—not the shrieks of Japanese but—the long, slow drawl of Australian men. I thought I was going troppo. But Sheila heard them too. She looked at me, amazed. We hadn't seen a Digger for months—men weren't allowed anywhere near our camp. Yet these were men all right. Singing Christmas carols. The whole camp went completely silent. Then women came running from everywhere—from bunks—from latrines—they even crawled out of the hospital hut. The Japs were waving rifles about but nobody cared. On the other side of our barbed wire fence were twenty or thirty Aussie men—as skinny as us—and wearing slouch hats. Unlike the Japs, they had hairy legs. And they were standing in rows—serenading us. We stood and watched—with only the barbed wire fence between us. One soldier waved—and winked at me. [*Pretending to be offended but actually very pleased*] Me—a nurse—the cheeky flirt. And when they'd finished, our choir sang back—

On the soundtrack, we hear a group of women singing 'God Rest Ye Merry Gentlemen'.

BRIDIE:— even though we were starving we were all in tune. And while we sang, there wasn't a war. There was only peace on earth. The Japs let us do it. I don't know why. [*The singing stops*] But soon the men were rounded up. They'd broken away from a working party—walked half a mile to be near our camp. They could have been shot, those boys. And the man who waved at me did it again! Utterly shameless. When they were gone, we went back to our rice. Sheila and I were both shaking from excitement. And Sheila said 'To hell with this! Let's have a proper Christmas dinner.' And she opened the tobacco tin—where we kept our precious caramel. She took it out and popped it in my mouth. We had one minute each until it was gone. I felt positively decadent. A wink and a caramel in one afternoon! For the first time in years I had a smile on my face.

I said 'Happy Christmas, Sheila'—and it was. It really was. A man had actually waved at me. When you're scrawny as a chicken—and you're dressed in rags—a wave from a bloke can be a pretty damn good present. As I drifted off to sleep I wondered about that soldier—and if I'd ever see him again.

M. VOICE: And did you?

BRIDIE: Yes. As a matter of fact I did. After the war I married him…

Blackout.

On the soundtrack we hear 'We'll Meet Again' performed by the Inkspots.

SCENE EIGHT

BRIDIE *and* SHEILA *are in* SHEILA*'s motel room. As the lights come up,* BRIDIE *is thrusting a glass of Alka Seltzer at a miserable looking* SHEILA, *who is wearing a dressing gown and gazing wretchedly at the fizzing water.*

BRIDIE: [*slightly impatient*] Stop staring and drink. It'll help your hangover.

SHEILA: [*defensively*] It's not a hangover—it's a headache. Was Rick very angry that I wasn't at the taping?

BRIDIE: He's surprised you're still alive… [*Calmly*] He was quite impressed by your party trick. We both were.

SHEILA: [*uneasily*] Party trick?

BRIDIE: Standing barefoot on a table singing 'God Save the King'—without your gloves.

SHEILA *groans.*

SHEILA: [*concerned*] Did I… talk about the camp?

BRIDIE: [*reassuringly*] No…

BRIDIE: [*before* SHEILA *can express relief*] You re-enacted it. [*Calmly*] For starters you told everyone that by the time we were liberated I'd forgotten how to use a cup and saucer.

SHEILA: [*trying to justify it*] Well it's true. You did. We hadn't seen them for years and—

SHEILA *looks at* BRIDIE, *then gulps down the Alka Seltzer.*

BRIDIE: [*calmly*] So you showed them how I buried my face—my snout as you called it—right in the cup—as if it were a rice bowl.

SHEILA: [*very worried*] Oh, Bridie— [*I'm sorry.*]

BRIDIE: Then you went on to describe our Welcome Home Morning Tea—how we ate the scones first and then had the butter.

SHEILA *groans again.*

BRIDIE: Oh the others were just as bad. Ava devoured a fish head. Raw. And Myra dissected a sanitary napkin to show how she used it to hide money from the Japs. Then the three of you formed a conga line—and moved off singing The Rice Song—wiggling your bottoms for the world and his wife.

SHEILA *looks up, embarrassed.*

BRIDIE: I am not judgemental, Sheila. But it looks a little like you might be over-fond of alcohol.

SHEILA: [*annoyed*] I do not have a drinking— [*Tries to stand up but it hurts, sits down again.*]— problem… Why didn't you stop me?

BRIDIE: [*calmly*] You pushed me away. [*Very calmly, almost laughing it off—but not quite.*] You told me not to come near you. Ever again.

SHEILA *looks at* BRIDIE *uneasily. Then she tries to change the subject.*

SHEILA: What did you talk about today—on camera?

BRIDIE: Christmas, 1943.

SHEILA: Oh yes… That little Australian boy—who asked us if Santa could bring him an egg—and died before we could find one.

BRIDIE: I didn't tell him that story. I refuse to cry in public… [*Calmly, but hurt.*] Why didn't you want to see me again? Are you upset because I married?

SHEILA: [*grimly*] Of course not. I'm happy for you.

BRIDIE: [*calmly*] Then why do you push me away?

SHEILA: Can't we just forget it?

BRIDIE: [*calmly*] We never had secrets in camp.

SHEILA: This isn't the camp.

BRIDIE: I hardly know anything about you now. I don't even know what your home is like or… how you've spent your life.

SHEILA: I look after books—like every librarian.

BRIDIE: [*politely, but with effort*] Do you garden? Do you bowl? [*Losing her patience*] Or do you sit at home and drink?

SHEILA: Spare me the lecture. You do not run my life.

BRIDIE: [*taking away the empty Alka Seltzer glass*] If I did, you wouldn't need that… [*Calmly, but hurt*] They say that a drunk always tells the truth. [*Trying to be light about it*] You were very drunk last night. You looked at me with hate and said: 'Don't come near me, Bridie.' [*Almost smiling fondly*] The look on your face. Everyone heard. They said it was funny and so did I. [*Muttering, trying to stay calm and tell it as an anecdote*] I was going to join the conga line. Sober and all I'd have acted the fool just for the sake of the old days. I walked up to you and that's when you said 'Don't come near me, Bridie.' [*Calmly*] Why did you push me away? Last night and… for fifty years?

SHEILA: [*defensively*] I wrote to you, remember?

BRIDIE: Once. In 1945—when I was still in a Singapore hospital bed. I got a note from you saying you were going off to England—and you'd send me your new address. I'm still waiting, Sheila. [*Hurt*] Why did you leave me?

SHEILA: [*not telling the truth*] All we had in common was the camp. I didn't want to keep talking about it—I couldn't, Bridie—it hurt too much. And when something hurts you run away… or you dig a hole and bury it.

BRIDIE: [*hurt*] Did you ever miss me—in all that time?

SHEILA: [*unsettled*] Of course.

BRIDIE: If you want to lie convincingly, don't look away when you speak… I couldn't believe you'd leave me when we'd been through so much together.

SHEILA: [*bitterly*] What did you expect—we'd all settle down in Chatswood—you, me and [*snidely*] Benny?

    BRIDIE *slaps* SHEILA.

BRIDIE: You're alive today because of me. And don't you ever forget it.

    By now SHEILA *cannot stop herself. She moves towards her bedside bureau and opens the drawer.*

SHEILA: I've spent fifty years trying to—if only I could! You want to know why I pushed you away. Here, Bridie—here's your answer.

SHEILA *takes the shoe-horn out of the drawer and throws it onto the bed.* BRIDIE *looks at it, puzzled, picks it up—and sees her initials.*

BRIDIE: [*stunned—and initially quite pleased*] Where did you get this? [*Looking at the initials*] It is mine—it is… But you swapped this. For quinine—when I came down with the fever.

SHEILA: Just take it and leave me alone.

BRIDIE: How did you get hold of it? Sheila? [*Puzzled and becoming angry*] I want to know how you got this back.

SHEILA: Do you remember the camp where you got sick?

BRIDIE: [*whispers*] Belalau.

SHEILA: Yes, Bridie. Belalau. The last place we were sent to. The camp nobody talks about. [*Almost in a threatening way*] Shall we talk about it now? Remember how pretty we thought it was? The frangipani everywhere—their perfume used to make us sick… And the beautiful sunsets—the mauves and the golds—and the columns of light in the sky after storms. And those nights. Filled with screams. As one by one the fever took them… [*Almost accusingly*] And you got it too.

BRIDIE: I remember.

SHEILA: [*angrily*] No you don't. You were too sick to remember anything… I cleaned you—tried to feed you—but you were spitting out the rice—and I knew what that meant—if you couldn't eat, you'd die. I had to do something.

BRIDIE: [*with concern and feeling threatened*] So you traded this. For quinine. But how did you get it back?

SHEILA: I took you to the hospital hut. But they said you wouldn't survive. Your skull was bursting from it. From cerebral malaria. I knelt down beside you and I… tried to hold you still but… you were shaking so much and… you pushed me away. Your eyes were dead and… your skin was clammy. I sang for you, Bridie, so you'd know I was there—that song you loved—the one you'd whistle. [*Muttering*] 'After the ball is over—after the break of morn.'

BRIDIE: [*calmly but with dread*] Where did you get the quinine tablets?

We hear the sound of crickets, distant at first, gradually getting louder as the scene continues.

SHEILA: Don't you see? I was scared. I hated those coffins—those awful bamboo boxes that the Japanese made us use—twenty women all struggling just to carry one between us. I wasn't going to carry you, Bridie. I couldn't let you die and leave me. I wouldn't have survived… So I went to the Japs—

BRIDIE: [*softly, frightened*] No…

SHEILA:— to Lipstick Larry 'cause he was always smiling at me. I took everything we owned—our tobacco tin—our hanky—and… your rotten bloody shoe-horn. And I showed him our things and… he laughed at them, Bridie… I don't really blame him. [*Looking at shoe-horn*] You couldn't melt this down for a bullet. And we could hear you screaming—even by the fence—and it wasn't a human sound by then—and Lipstick Larry said 'Plenty of room in the graveyard for her.' Outside I could see our Red Cross supplies—the ones that the Japanese stacked beyond the wire—where we could never, ever reach them… Oh Lipstick Larry knew what I wanted. 'Nice girl,' he said. I was skin and bone by then but—there was prestige for a Jap if a—a white girl went off with him.

BRIDIE: You didn't. Tell me you didn't.

SHEILA: [*angrily*] You were the one who wanted to know. I told you to leave it alone.

BRIDIE: [*shocked*] You didn't sleep with a Jap. Not you.

SHEILA: You were screaming. And he went and got quinine. For you. And he showed the tablets to me—and he pointed to the barracks—where his mates were waiting.

BRIDIE: Don't! I don't want to hear this!

SHEILA: Their cheeks were pink from too much saki—I couldn't look them in the eye so I… stared at their boots—their webbed-toe boots—and they told me to sing—and when I did, they cried. Like little boys. And I thought 'They'll let me go. If men can cry, they'll let me go. They won't try and make me.' And I crept to the door— but they saw me, Bridie. They saw me and they dragged me back.

BRIDIE: [*whispers*] No… no…

> BRIDIE *stares at* SHEILA *in shock. The noise of crickets ceases.*

SHEILA: All these years I've told myself that you'd have done the same for me. [*Calmly*] I was wrong, though, wasn't I?

BRIDIE: Sheila—

SHEILA: You said you'd let your family die before you'd give in to the Japs. Did you mean it? Is it true?

BRIDIE *does not reply.*

SHEILA: Answer me, Bridie? [*Firmly*] Don't look away. You can't tell the truth if you look away… Would you have gone to the Japs for me?

BRIDIE *still faces away from* SHEILA. *Both of them are isolated in spotlights. On the soundtrack we hear* YOUNG SHEILA*'s voice.*

Y. SHEILA: [*v/o*] Bridie? Bridie, love—it's me. Look—I've got tablets. I sold your shoe-horn. I've got tablets. [*Gently*] Come on now— try and swallow them… Don't leave me, Bridie. Please don't leave me…

Very slowly BRIDIE *turns to face* SHEILA. *Her answer is obvious.*

The lights slowly fade.

[*v/o sings very gently*] 'After the ball is over/ after the break of morn/ after the dancers leaving/ after the stars are gone/ many a heart is aching/ if you could read them all/ many the hopes that have vanished/ after the ball… '

END OF ACT ONE

ACT TWO

The 'On Air' sign lights up. Projected onto the screen is a photograph of row upon row of captured British and Australian women bowing to the Japanese. The photograph is huge. It fills the screen. It remains in view.

> BRIDIE, *standing on one side of the stage, begins to sing. She is accompanied by an unseen Women's Choir.*

BRIDIE: [*singing*] Father in captivity/ We would lift our prayer to Thee./ Keep us ever in Thy Love,/ Grant that daily we may prove/ Those who place their trust in Thee/ More than conquerors may be.

> *We become aware that* SHEILA *is sitting at the other side of the stage—in front of the camera.*

SHEILA: [*smiling as she remembers*] Oh yes—It's called The Captives' Hymn. We sang it every Sunday—well almost every Sunday. We had to stop towards the end of the war.

M. VOICE: Why? Why did you stop?

SHEILA: Half our choir had died—and the rest of us were too weak to sing... You see in April 1945 the Japs had decided to move us. They took us from our camp at Muntok and shifted us inland—to a place called... Belalau.

> BRIDIE *and* SHEILA *exchange an uneasy look.*

[*quite calmly*] Not many people have heard of Belalau. [*Almost pleasantly*] Oh it wasn't the site of any big battle. It wasn't important at all—except to us. Belalau was just a rubber plantation— [*with a trace of fear*] completely cut off from the outside world. We went there by boat—by a cattle boat. It was moored at the end of a pier... But this pier stretched out for half a mile. And we had to walk it—hundreds of women who could barely stand up, dragging their children behind them. Our legs all wobbly from beri beri— we looked like drunks coming home from a party—in coolie hats and tattered rags and our worldly goods slung over our shoulders. The sick and the dying were left behind—uncovered—in the sun. I kept telling Bridie I couldn't go on—and Bridie kept saying 'Stop whinging, girl!' as she put her arm around my waist and dragged me to that boat.

BRIDIE: [*singing*] Give us patience to endure,/ Keep our hearts serene and pure,/ Grant us courage, charity,/ Greater faith, humility./ Readiness to own Thy will/ Be we free or captive still.

SHEILA: We were now the kind of people one would never have let into Raffles—dirty beggars, destitute women, grubby, thieving children. They shoved us in the cargo hold—no food, no water, no space to lie down. And no toilets of course, though we all had dysentery. The Australian nurses were quite unfazed—as if this were the way one travelled Down Under. They immediately tied some handles to their rice pots—and announced that now we had bedpans. Then one of the nurses spent the whole of the trip hanging off a six inch ledge—emptying out and rinsing these pans. The Japanese watched her and laughed—and waited for her to fall into the water. They'd have let her drown—and she knew it. The nurse was pitifully thin and weak but... she held on there for hours. She kept on saying that we weren't animals... and she'd rather die than be treated like one. It was the bravest act I have ever seen. She didn't get a medal for it but... all of us loved her for that... The cargo hold was stiflingly hot and the old and the frail began to die. The Japs then dumped them overboard—and they floated right beside us. We could hear their bodies as they knocked against the boat...

BRIDIE: [*singing*] May the day of freedom dawn./ Peace and justice be reborn./ Grant that nations Loving Thee/ O'er the world may brothers be/ Cleansed by suffering, know rebirth,/ See Thy kingdom come on earth.

SHEILA: What none of us knew was that all over Asia thousands of prisoners were on the move.

M. VOICE: Why did they move you?

SHEILA: Because an order had been issued by the Japanese Command. Every prisoner of war—man, woman and child—was to die by October 1945. By bullet or sword or hunger or poison. They were taking us inland—where we'd never be found.

M. VOICE: Did you know—about the Order?

SHEILA: We guessed. You develop a sense for these things as a prisoner. The guards who'd been kind kept away from us now. And the cruel ones became ever crueller. Oh yes, the end was coming. We could smell it on the wind... By now our songs were of a less uplifting kind.

BRIDIE: [*chants*] One day I killed a Jap/ Killed a Jap./ I hit him on the head/ With a bloody lump of lead./ Blast his soul./ Damn his eyes./ Bloody hell.

> *The huge photograph of bowing women fades.* BRIDIE *leaves the stage.*

SHEILA: The Japs introduced a new rule at Belalau—No work, no food. So if you were sick and couldn't get up, you were left to starve to death. We agreed to share our food with the sick but... not all the women would. Soon there were fights—oh the Japs loved those—watching us squabble over scraps and bones and fish heads.

M. VOICE: There must have been edible fruit in the jungle.

SHEILA: [*slightly irritated*] You think we didn't know that? Bananas grew everywhere—all round the camp. On our way to work we'd walk past hundreds. But the Japs wouldn't let us pick a single one. So we watched them rot before our eyes.

M. VOICE: You say you worked. What sort of work?

SHEILA: Grave-digging mostly. We were too weak to stand—let alone use a hoe—so we'd get down on all fours—Bridie would hack at the earth with her shoe-horn—and I'd rake it back with my hands. We became quite skilled at digging these pits. Different sizes for different people and... smaller ones for children. But soon demand had outstripped supply. Four graves a day were required. Grave-digging wasn't too bad a job actually—apart from spiders, snakes and scorpions. It was a shame we had to stop.

M. VOICE: Why did you give it up?

SHEILA: One morning—in July—I had trouble waking Bridie. I told her she'd be late for tenko. And she said she'd be there when she'd fed the chooks. We didn't have chooks—let alone chook-feed. She was pale and shaking and... I knew what it was. Cerebral malaria. Always fatal—unless you had medicine. Now the Japs had quinine—they had mountains of the stuff. But because they'd been ordered to wipe us out, they wouldn't give us any. By mid-day Bridie didn't even know me and—so I—

She hesitates, as if about to tell what really happened, then overcomes the impulse.

— I went to this guard—we called him Lipstick Larry.

M. VOICE: Why?

SHEILA: If he saw a woman wearing lipstick, he'd punch her in the face. But he... wasn't such a bad chap. I didn't have much to offer him. Just my old tobacco tin... and Bridie's shoe-horn. He took pity on me. A rare thing for a Jap. I swapped that shoe-horn for some quinine tablets. And Bridie got better.

M. VOICE: So that shoe-horn ended up saving you both? You in the sea—and Bridie in camp.

SHEILA: [*slightly uneasy*] Yes, I... suppose it did.

M. VOICE: Did you know much about the progress of the war?

SHEILA: Only what the Japs would tell us—and that wasn't always reliable. Once they announced that their submarines had sunk the Sydney Harbour Bridge. 'Dad'll be pleased,' Bridie muttered. 'He reckons that bridge ruined Chatswood.'

M. VOICE: All this time did you ever hear from your government?

SHEILA: Not the English. No. But the Australians did. The Japs passed on a message once. Just after Bridie got back on her feet, Captain Siki called a line up. He said: 'I have good news for Australian womens. Your Emperor, Mr Curtin, sends his greetings. And orders you all to keep smiling.' At first there was... absolute silence. And then the nurses— [*Slightly puzzled*]— well I thought they must be crying—because they started to wipe their eyes. But it was from laughter. They were laughing.

M. VOICE: Why? What was so funny?

SHEILA: They were skin and bone and covered in boils—and they'd just been told to 'keep smiling'! Well they smiled all right. Then they laughed so much they couldn't control it. Siki slapped a few faces and they managed to stop. But all that day you could hear these giggles as the joke went right round the camp. There was even laughter after bed time—instead of the usual sobbing and quarrels.

The guards would bark and shine their torches—and all would be quiet till some wit muttered 'Keep smiling, girls!'—and we'd all crack up. We paid dearly for our fun though. The next day Siki lined us up. He made us stand in the sun for hours—and ordered us never to smile again...

> *Darkness. Two photographs of war-time Prime Minister John Curtin appear on the screen. He looks quite distressed. These are followed by two photographs of emaciated male prisoners of war, starving, dying, and covered in tropical ulcers. On the soundtrack we hear Judy Garland singing 'When You're Smiling'...*

SCENE TEN

The photograph of starving male prisoners remains in view. The lights come up to show SHEILA *sitting beneath (or near) this photograph, doing tapestry (or some kind of needle-work) with great intensity. She is wearing her small microphone.* SHEILA *barely looks up when* BRIDIE *enters.*

BRIDIE: [*clipping on her microphone*] Canteen's closing.

> SHEILA *does not reply.*

BRIDIE: [*more pointedly*] You're missing lunch.

SHEILA: [*without looking up*] It's a risotto. You know I can't stand rice.

> BRIDIE *looks up at the photograph.*

BRIDIE: We were thinner than that.

SHEILA: [*reproachfully*] There aren't any photos of us, remember. [*Calmly but accusingly*] Your army wouldn't allow them till we'd all been fattened up a bit.

BRIDIE: [*defensively but not with complete sincerity*] I'm glad of it too. If my Dad had seen what I looked like then, he'd have probably had a heart attack... I'll forgive the Japs a lot of things but those rotten buggers ruined my bosom.

> BRIDIE *peers at the tapestry.*

That's the wrong colour there.

SHEILA *glares at* BRIDIE, *then continues to stitch resolutely.*

BRIDIE: [*nervously but trying to sound calm*] Rick says he'll finish up tomorrow. So I guess we'll be going home... Are you sure you'll be all right?

SHEILA: I've managed quite well for the past fifty years.

BRIDIE: Do you... live on your own?

SHEILA: [*defensively*] Who doesn't at our age?

BRIDIE: [*trying to be tactful*] Has it always been like that?

SHEILA: You mean 'Did I ever have lovers?' What do you think, Bridie? [*Not wanting pity*] I didn't really mind. Mother always used to say that sex was like a trip to Brighton. Took you ages to get there and it wasn't worth the trouble. Even she drew the line at doing it for England.

BRIDIE: [*with concern*] If there's anything you ever need—any way I can help—

SHEILA: [*tersely*] You can help by trying to behave yourself. I saw what you were having for lunch. Cheesecake and cream—no wonder you get heartburn.

BRIDIE: [*defensively*] You're worse than Jenny Bloody Craig. I am perfectly entitled to a few years of stress-eating after what I've found out.

SHEILA: [*wearily*] Oh Bridie, don't start.

BRIDIE: You're right. I won't. No point in getting upset now. I'm fifty years too late for that.

BRIDIE *takes some Mylanta from her purse, shakes the bottle, then has a swig from it.*

BRIDIE: If only I'd know in '45. Why didn't you tell me sooner?

SHEILA: [*uneasily*] I tried.

BRIDIE: [*angrily*] When? When did you try?

SHEILA: Just after we were rescued—in that hospital in Singapore. The first few nights we couldn't sleep 'cause our beds were too soft— and we weren't used to sheets... So you talked about Chatswood— every street in Chatswood. And I lay there listening... with your shoe-horn hidden under my pillow. I wanted to tell you—I wanted to so much but—

BRIDIE: Why the hell didn't you?

SHEILA: Because you'd had a chest X-ray. And the doctor said with a bit of luck you might survive for another five years. I'd always thought of you as strong. I never guessed that you were dying.

BRIDIE: [*dismissively*] Takes more than TB to get me.

SHEILA: What would it have taken Bridie? If I'd told you the truth then, would the shock have killed you? I couldn't risk it, don't you see? And I couldn't stay and keep on lying. So as soon as I could walk I... left.

BRIDIE: [*hurt*] Without so much as a word of farewell.

SHEILA: I waited till you were fast asleep—then I stood by your bed for a couple of minutes. [*Sadly, tenderly*] You looked so peaceful lying there, smelling of talc, your hair combed back. I wanted to wake you—and tell you everything—just like I always did in camp. But I couldn't—you were too sick... For the first time in years I was on my own... I said 'Good-bye, Bridie'—and I kissed you on the cheek.

BRIDIE: And off you went to a new life in England.

SHEILA: Mother said I was mad to leave Singapore. She and Daddy stayed on as if nothing had happened. I hopped off the ship at its first port of call. I didn't care where I was. All I wanted was... to get away from war. [*Calmly*] And I got used to Australia in time. But there were certain things I could not get used to... I could not get used to walking around without seeing your shadow beside me. And I could not get used to saying 'Good night'—and not hearing your voice in reply.

BRIDIE: [*upset*] Why did you have to go with that Jap?

SHEILA: Ssshh!

BRIDIE: You were only a girl—a child!

SHEILA: I had to do it. I couldn't let you die.

BRIDIE: If only I'd known—I would never have let you... Sheila— please—let me try and help.

SHEILA: [*haunted*] Every night when I fall asleep, Lipstick Larry's waiting. He calls to me and I go to him—and no one can change that. Not even you.

BRIDIE: Have you told anyone else?

SHEILA: I almost confided in mother once. [*Sadly*] Isn't that amusing? It was just before I sailed from Singapore. I took her hand and whispered that... there was something I needed to tell her—about the Japanese. Mother poured herself a drink and said: 'You know what the Bible says, my dear. "No cross, no crown." We must pull up our socks and get on with it.' Took more than a war to change Mother.

BRIDIE: [*upset and annoyed*] I tried so hard to protect you—to get you out alive and untouched.

SHEILA: [*bitterly*] But I let you down, didn't I?

BRIDIE: [*angrily*] Yes. You did! You ruined your life—

Pause.

[*vehemently*]... for a Jap!

SHEILA: [*angrily*] I did it for you. I was stupid enough to think that you'd have done the same for me.

BRIDIE: I'd have starved for you. Died for you. Anything but...

SHEILA: [*finishing the sentence*] But that. You'd never have done what I did for you.

Pause.

BRIDIE *looks at* SHEILA.

[*calmly, almost brightly*] Well—tomorrow I'll be going—so we'll be out of each other's way.

BRIDIE: [*distressed*] Oh—Sheila—

SHEILA: Now don't get maudlin on me. I'll be perfectly all right. 'No cross, no crown', remember.

BRIDIE: [*sadly, earnestly*] You should have let me die.

SHEILA: Yes. Perhaps I should have.

They glare at each other for several seconds. A MALE VOICE *cuts in before* BRIDIE *can reply.*

M. VOICE: [*brightly*] Hello, ladies! Did you have a nice lunch?

BRIDIE *and* SHEILA *look up, startled. Then they both realise they are wearing small microphones. They both wonder whether every word has been overheard. On the soundtrack we hear Anne Shelton singing 'I'll Walk Alone'.*

SCENE ELEVEN

The red 'On Air' sign lights up. BRIDIE *and* SHEILA *are sitting side by side.* BRIDIE *is holding up a small, square piece of cardboard.*

BRIDIE: This arrived in 1944. A Red Cross postcard. With a twenty word limit.

SHEILA: The only letters we ever had—

BRIDIE: And dated 1942! [It] Took the Japs two years to deliver their mail. Still it was wonderful to get this. Our families didn't know if we were even alive. Six million civilians had been killed by the Japs. So the odds weren't good. But they wrote to us anyway.

SHEILA: We sat in the dust and read our postcards—over and over. Laughing and crying at memories of home.

BRIDIE: And then we read each other's till we knew them off by heart.

   SHEILA *points to* BRIDIE*'s postcard and recites its contents from memory.*

SHEILA: 'Mum and Gran send hugs and kisses. The chooks haven't laid since you left. Love Dad.'

   BRIDIE *does likewise with* SHEILA*'s postcard—with some comic impersonation.*

BRIDIE: 'Raffles bombed. Daddy devastated—'

   SHEILA *joins in for the last few words.*

BOTH: 'Chin up. Mother.'

   Darkness for a few seconds.

BRIDIE: In April, 1945, dear Miss Dryburgh passed away. Well the choir just couldn't go on without her—more than half of our singers had already died—so we decided to disband. It was hard to get used to a life without singing. Sheila and I both felt pretty low. Then a little while after—in the middle of the night—Sheila shook me awake and whispered— [*With intensity*] 'What do Bach and Beethoven have in common?'

SHEILA: The look on Bridie's face! She thought I'd come down with the fever.

BRIDIE: [*defensively*] I wasn't trained in music.

M. VOICE: Well—what do they have in common?

BRIDIE: They both wrote sonatas.

SHEILA: A sonata is—

BRIDIE: [*peeved at this interruption*] I'm perfectly capable of telling him. [*To camera*] The sonata is a piece for two musical instruments.

SHEILA: Or voices representing instruments... We both still had voices—Bridie and I—and since the choir couldn't sing any more, it was up to us to carry on. Miss Dryburgh would have wanted that.

BRIDIE: Sheila worked out a medley—

SHEILA: A sonata, Bridie, please.

BRIDIE: Two voices. Four movements—'Für Elise', 'Country Garden', 'Humoresque', and 'Danny Boy'.

SHEILA: We'd sit in our huts at night and hum. We'd do it while we dug the graves.

BRIDIE: When I had the strength I'd tap out the rhythm—waving the shoe-horn—not as grandly as before.

SHEILA: A lot of times we barely got through it—we were so weak from hunger. But we sang our sonata whenever we could—so the camp would know there was still music left.

BRIDIE: It probably sounded bloody awful. But not to us. To us we still had harmony... and the Japs could never ever take that away.

Darkness for a few seconds.

SHEILA: [*calmly and without a trace of self-pity*] Once, in my holidays—I went back to the camp. I'd spent thirty years running away from it—not telling a soul—trying to forget. And then I went back. The huts are gone—the wire—the fences. The grass has swallowed everything. The taxi driver thought I was crazy—pacing about in the jungle. But I was trying to find our cemetery—where I'd buried all my friends—Marguerite, my chum from school, Mrs Coombs, who taught me piano... and dear Miss Dryburgh.

M. VOICE: [*surprised and a little shocked*] They're not still there—the bodies, I mean?

SHEILA: Oh yes. They removed the remains of the army nurses—but they left the women and children behind. There are more than three hundred of them buried in that jungle. Not a headstone or memorial anywhere. Not even a cross survived the war. We were 'useless mouths' in death as well.

M. VOICE: [*gently*] Why did you go back?

SHEILA: Because I'd never really left...

> *Darkness for a few seconds.* BRIDIE *stands beside* SHEILA *and addresses the camera.*

BRIDIE: [*calmly*] In 1951 we were each sent thirty pounds. The Japanese said it was compensation. That's sixpence a day for each day of imprisonment.

SHEILA: We've tried to fight for more but... the government has opposed us.

M. VOICE: You mean the Japanese government?

BRIDIE: No. The Australian government. They told us we were on our own. Just like they told us once to keep smiling.

> *Darkness.*

> *On the soundtrack we hear Alice Faye singing 'You'll Never Know How Much I Love You'.*

SCENE TWELVE

BRIDIE *and* SHEILA *have just returned from the TV Studio. As they enter the motel room, they are in the middle of an animated discussion.*

BRIDIE: I could take you to Balmoral. We could stroll along the beach.

SHEILA: We'd spend the whole time bickering.

BRIDIE: That's the most ridiculous thing I've—

SHEILA: [*calmly but not with confidence*] And I won't let you harangue me till you get your own way. I'm a grown woman now with a will of my own.

BRIDIE: [*annoyed*] Oh you always had that, my girl. [The] First time I saw you—splashing in the water—I knew you'd either drown or be difficult.

SHEILA: [*defensively*] That's not fair. I was perfectly polite.

BRIDIE: Insisting Frank Sinatra was better than Bing Crosby.

SHEILA: You agreed—in the end.

BRIDIE: It was the biggest lie I've ever told. I was trying to keep you afloat.

SHEILA: [*annoyed, and making tea*] A weekend with you would be disastrous for us both. You'll never approve of me, Bridie, and—

BRIDIE: When have I ever disapproved?

> SHEILA *glares at* BRIDIE. *Then* BRIDIE *reaches for the Tim Tams.*

SHEILA: [*looking at the biscuit*] You shouldn't eat those. What about your cholesterol?

BRIDIE: [*glumly and defiantly*] Eight point six and I don't care... [*Hurt*] I didn't think we'd be like this—snapping at each other after all these years.

SHEILA: [*placatingly as she pours tea*] Well we're not the only ones. Irene and Joyce had a blue last night. Then Joyce got drunk and told the Chinese waiter she forgave him for all his war-time atrocities.

BRIDIE: [*amused*] Really?

> BRIDIE *and* SHEILA *look at each other and smile. There is peace—for the moment.*

SHEILA: [*wistfully*] If only the Japs hadn't bombed our ships—we'd have both got away and—things would have been different. Do you still hate them for it?

BRIDIE: [*shaking her head*] Not now... Now they just terrify me... The most benign looking tourist gives me palpitations for hours.

SHEILA: You weren't afraid of the guards in camp.

BRIDIE: I was petrified.

SHEILA: [*surprised*] Really?

BRIDIE: I had to look brave—for both our sakes ...

> *She hesitates.*

[*trying to sound casual but concealing great effort*] I got arrested once—because of the Nips.

> SHEILA, *who has been drinking her tea, almost chokes when she hears this.*

I should never have told you. I knew you'd be shocked.

SHEILA: I'm not. Honestly.

BRIDIE: Then why are you dribbling?

SHEILA: [*wiping her mouth*] What on earth did you do?

No reply. BRIDIE *munches glumly on a Tim Tam.*

SHEILA: Bridie?

BRIDIE: [*reluctantly and embarrassed*] I left a store without paying for something.

SHEILA: [*surprised*] You shoplifted?

BRIDIE: [*defensively*] There was a—misunderstanding—in the David Jones Food Hall. I had just selected a tin of shortbread when this bus load of Japanese tourists arrived. Well in no time at all they had practically surrounded me. Oh I knew they were harmless—and perfectly polite—but my heart began to pound with terror. Just hearing the language was enough to do it. I couldn't breathe—and I… started to shake. So I ran. Outside. Still clutching the tin—or 'Exhibit A' as the cops later called it… I was treated like a common criminal. They wouldn't even let me put on make-up for the mug shots…

SHEILA: But didn't you explain that—

BRIDIE: I… pleaded guilty.

SHEILA: [*exasperated*] Bridie.

BRIDIE: If I'd told them about the camp, they'd have checked up with the army. And the whole nursing corps would have known in a week… So instead I went to Court. [*In mortified disbelief*] I had to stand in front of a judge.

SHEILA: But didn't he ask why you'd done it?

BRIDIE: [*nodding*] I said it was change of life, and I was let off with a fine. Thank God they never found out in Chatswood…

SHEILA'*s face is quite expressionless.*

Well don't just look at me. Say something.

SHEILA: Were the shortbread nice?

BRIDIE: Sheila!

SHEILA: [*putting her arm around* BRIDIE] It isn't so terrible, love.

BRIDIE: It's the end of the world for me… I still lie awake at night cringing with shame— [*in disbelief*]— my photo in a police mug book—cheek to cheek with Neddie Smith!… I'll forgive the Japs for what they did to us in camp—but I'll never forgive them for the David Jones Food Hall… [*With regret*] I shouldn't have mentioned it. I promised myself I'd never tell anyone.

SHEILA: [*reassuringly*] I'm not just anyone, Bridie. [*Thinking of them both*] Keeping a secret wears you down. Believe me—I know. In the end you'll do anything just to escape it. That's why those women went public I suppose—the ones who had to work in the Japanese army brothels. I sometimes wish I could talk about it.

BRIDIE: [*uneasily*] You have. You've told me.

SHEILA: I don't see why it... should have to be a secret. Not now.

BRIDIE: [*unnerved*] You mustn't discuss it beyond this room. You know how cruel other people can be. It's the only thing that hasn't changed in the last fifty years. What on earth has possessed you to—

SHEILA: [*haunted*] When I went back to Belalau—searching for the graves—I kept on thinking, why did they die? Was it all for nothing? All our friends? And that's when I realised I had to talk about it. There are probably thousands of survivors like us—still trapped in the war—too ashamed to tell anyone. Lots of people will be watching when Rick's programme goes to air. It mightn't be too late to—

BRIDIE: [*upset and threatened*] To what? [*Do*] You think the armies of this planet will stop murdering each other because some old English woman disapproves of all the killing?

    SHEILA *shakes her head sadly.*

Then what possible difference will it make?

SHEILA: [*haunted but gently*] Probably none. I know that, Bridie. But the war hasn't ended. Not for me. For me it goes on. And now I want peace. And if the only way to get it is to tell the truth then—

BRIDIE: You were always impulsive and you haven't changed since camp. [*Bitterly*] This is what Rick's been after all along, I'll bet. This is why the free booze and the room with ocean views. He's been softening us up. Can't you see that, Sheila?

SHEILA: And what if he has? It's still my decision.

BRIDIE: You know what they'll call you. They'll call you a whore.

SHEILA: [*stung*] Not every place on earth is as intolerant as Chatswood.

BRIDIE: [*defensively*] Chatswood happens to be a most sophisticated suburb.

SHEILA: [*every inch a woman of the Empire*] Sophisticated people do not keep chooks.

BRIDIE: [*calmly picking up her Tim Tams*] If I'd known you were going to behave like this, I'd have let you drown in the South China Sea. Good night.

> *As* BRIDIE *exits,* SHEILA *follows her to the door. Exasperated and angry,* SHEILA *makes chicken noises.*

SHEILA: [*waving her arms like wings*] Buck-buck-buck-buck-buck-buck-buck. Bawk-buck-buck-buck-buck-buck-buck! Damn you, Bridie. Damn you!

> *Darkness.*

> *Photographs of war-time political leaders appear on the screen. We see the faces of Churchill, Hitler, Mussolini, Stalin and Mao. On the soundtrack we hear the Ink Spots singing 'Whispering Grass'—a 1940's song about a secret and forbidden love.*

SCENE THIRTEEN

The red 'On Air' sign lights up.

BRIDIE: From April 1945, the Japs began raiding our huts. Ransacking everything—searching for diaries. They wanted no records of what they'd been doing. When a diary was found, its owner was bashed and locked in a bamboo cage. Few survived that. But women went on writing them. They scrawled on cardboard—bits of paper— anything at all—while we kept watch.

M. VOICE: Weren't you foolish to run such a risk?

BRIDIE: Yes. And desperate. Those diaries were our only hope. We thought if the Japs ever murdered us all, some of our scribbling might be found one day—and our families would know... why we hadn't come home... and how we never stopped thinking about them.

SHEILA: After the war, when we were rescued, the British asked if they could borrow our diaries. Just for an hour. So they could fumigate them. Most women obliged. But a few—out of habit— continued to hide them. Those women were wise. The British didn't want anyone to know about us. They'd have lost prestige if people found out how the women of their Empire had lived in the war. So for the sake of King and Country, they burned our diaries. Every last one.

On the screen we see a photograph of the atomic bomb that destroyed Hiroshima—the infamous mushroom cloud. This is followed by a photograph of the devastated city.

BRIDIE *looks at the camera.*

BRIDIE: Eight army nurses died in Belalau in the final months of the war. The last one to go was... Pearl Mittelhauser. With a name like that, we had to call her Mitzi... For a week we'd begged the Japs for quinine. But their response was always the same. 'Plenty of room in the graveyard.' Mitzi died on the 18th of August, 1945.

M. VOICE: [*slightly surprised*] You mean she died when the war was over? It had ended on the fifteenth.

BRIDIE: Not for us it hadn't. Oh the guards must have known—but they weren't letting on. For them it was business as usual—starving us, bashing us, withholding the quinine. And more and more women perished every day.

M. VOICE: Didn't the Allies know where you were?

SHEILA: The Japs wanted our camp kept a secret—in case they were charged with war crimes. So they told the Allies we'd all been drowned—back in 1942! Only our guards knew we were alive— and they'd begun to dig a mass grave.

M. VOICE: Did you really believe that they'd wipe you out?

SHEILA: Oh yes. Absolutely. The Japanese were quite open about it. They'd look at us and say 'Marti! Marti!'—'Dead! Dead!'

BRIDIE: One morning—towards the end—we were woken up by soldiers, screaming and pounding on the walls of our huts. 'All womens out! All womens out!' They rounded up everybody—the sick—the dying—the children.

SHEILA: We were told to climb to the top of this hill. It sounds so easy—but it took us ages. Hundreds of us—struggling to get up that slope—some on all fours—crawling through the grass. The guards were running up and down—shrieking—and waving their bayonets. 'Speedo, womens! Speedo!' [*A hint of emotion is starting to show*] We knew they'd be waiting at the top with machine guns. And... as we got closer—

SHEILA *has trouble continuing.*

[*softly to* BRIDIE]— you finish will you?

BRIDIE: [*taking* SHEILA*'s hand*] I took Sheila's hand... and we started to pray—'The Lord is my shepherd. I shall not want. He maketh me—'

SHEILA *joins in.*

BOTH: '— to lie down in green pastures. He leadeth me beside the still waters …'

BRIDIE: At the top of the hill there were thirty more Japs. Thirty Japs we'd never seen. All lined up in full dress uniform. I assumed they were some sort of Death Squad. I started searching for somewhere to hide—a patch of grass where the Japs mightn't see us. And that was when I heard Sheila say—'Oh God. Oh, Bridie—look! Look!'

SHEILA: That's right. I did.

BRIDIE: [*to* SHEILA] See. I do remember some things... [*Calmly to the camera*] I thought she must have seen the guns. I hurried to her side—so that we could die together... But these Japanese soldiers didn't carry weapons. These Japs had trumpets.

SHEILA: Trumpets—drums—clarinets—trombones. They were a band. An army brass band. We didn't know whether to laugh or cry.

On the soundtrack we hear the beginning of 'The Blue Danube' by J. Strauss. It continues throughout the following speeches.

And there—in the jungle—for hundreds of starving women and children—the Japanese played 'The Blue Danube Waltz'. And they were wonderful.

BRIDIE: It was music we'd danced to—with husbands and boyfriends and soldiers long dead... And everyone was humming and crying... [*still amazed*] and the trombones and trumpets were shining in the sunlight—and these men—these men in their clean white uniforms—

SHEILA: We hadn't seen anything clean for years.

The waltz continues on the soundtrack—joyous, triumphant— the music of life.

BRIDIE: And we looked at the sky—at the clouds—and the birds. And I took Sheila's hand—and I squeezed it so hard. 'We're going to live,' I said to her. [*With great determination—as the waltz reaches a crescendo*] 'I don't care how or what it takes, we are going to survive this war. And when it's over, you and I will go dancing. We will. I know we will.'

More music, then it gradually fades.

SHEILA: They played for two hours. Then Captain Siki stood on a box and shouted—'The Geneva Convention says: All prisoners must have culture. You womens have just had yours.'

BRIDIE: And Sheila leaned over and whispered to me: 'I wouldn't be at all surprised if the Japs are losing this war!'

M. VOICE: Did you two ever go dancing?

BRIDIE is very moved by this recollection.

BRIDIE: [*with regret*] No. We didn't.

M. VOICE: So how were you found?

BRIDIE: By luck. Or a miracle. An Australian journalist kept hearing these rumours—native rumours that no one believed—about a secret camp in the depths of the jungle. He began to search Sumatra—just on the off-chance. And he found us on the 24th of August...

A blink of light.

Photographs of Australians celebrating peace appear on the screen—ticker-tape parades and dancing crowds in Martin Place, Sydney. On the soundtrack we hear Glen Miller's Orchestra playing 'Danny Boy'—it is a slightly jazzed-up version and its sound is both poignant and joyous.

On August 26th 1945, the Japanese fled from Belalau—and the gates of our camp were left wide open—for the first time in over three years.

SHEILA: One thousand two hundred and eighty seven days.

BRIDIE: We stood and looked at the dusty road that led down to a village. And I said to Sheila 'Fancy a stroll?' But she shook her head. 'Go on,' I said. 'We'll just take a few steps. If we don't like it out there, we can always come back.'... And I took Sheila's hand and we... walked to the gate...

SHEILA: [*nervously*] My knees were shaking—I was—terribly frightened. I said 'What if the Japs come after us, Bridie?' [*Smiling sadly*] I remember her words so clearly. 'And what if they do?' she said. 'Since when have we ever been scared of the Japs?'

BRIDIE *reaches out and takes* SHEILA*'s hand.*

BRIDIE: So Sheila and I walked out of that camp. [*Gently, fondly, perhaps smiling sadly*] And on four wobbly legs we went down to the village. Sometimes I dragged Sheila. Sometimes Sheila dragged me. The main thing is we got there. And we could never have done that alone.

M. VOICE: We can have a break now if you like.

SHEILA *is about to agree when* BRIDIE *interrupts.*

SHEILA: Yes—that would be—

BRIDIE: [*firmly*] I want to go on.

SHEILA: Bridie—

BRIDIE: [*looking at camera*] We've left out something. Something important. One day in July—1945—before the war ended—I woke up with a headache. A very bad headache. There was no doubt what it was. Cerebral malaria. [*Shaking her head sadly*] So much for my hopes of getting home... Soon my skull was bursting—I was screaming from the pain. And I knew I was going to die... I would have too—except for Sheila. I'm here today because of her.

SHEILA: [*calmly*] It wasn't such a big thing. I've already told you—I—I went to one of the Japanese guards and I... swapped Bridie's shoe-horn for some quinine tablets. She would have survived anyway. The woman's as strong as an ox.

BRIDIE: [*calmly to* SHEILA] That isn't the truth, love... [*Very gently*] Do you want me to tell the truth?

SHEILA *hesitates, looks at* BRIDIE *with both fear and gratitude.*

Pause.

SHEILA *nods.* BRIDIE *reaches out and takes* SHEILA*'s hand.*

She went to... the Japs... to a Japanese guard—and... she sold herself to him for tablets. She was a beautiful, kind and brave young woman. [*Looking at* SHEILA.] She wasn't just my friend—she was—she is—the other half of my life. And she gave herself to him... so that I... could have quinine... And she never told me till two nights ago. For fifty years she never told anyone... They don't give medals for things like that. But they should.

Squeezes SHEILA*'s hand and tries to smile gently.*

Now I want you to tell them about the David Jones Food Hall.

SHEILA: [*reluctantly*] But Bridie—

BRIDIE: [*gently but firmly*] Go on, dear.

SHEILA: Bridie borrowed a packet of shortbread biscuits.

BRIDIE: It was a tin. I stole a tin. And I was arrested. In the David Jones Food Hall. I'm not complaining. They were doing their job.

SHEILA: [*defensively*] It wasn't Bridie's fault. Some Japanese tourists scared her—the sound of their voices—chattering away—well it brought it all back. [*Almost fiercely*] But if I'd been there it wouldn't have happened. I wouldn't have let those policemen get near her. [*Very tenderly*] Bridie Cartwright was the best—the best nurse— the best thief—the best woman in our camp. And I'd do it all over again if I had to. [*Firmly*] I'd go to those Japs and I wouldn't think twice—'cause Bridie's my friend—and that's all there is to it...

Gradual darkness.

On the soundtrack we hear 'An Epitaph to War'—a short, poignant hymn performed by a choir of young boys. Now we see photos of the Australian Army nurses recuperating in hospital. They are thin and sick—but alive. We see them sharing food, talking, getting their hair set, lying in beds with clean sheets and blankets.

Finally we see the famous photograph of the Australian Army nurses arriving in Singapore after their rescue from Belalau. Only twenty-four of the sixty-five have survived. They are all emaciated—but smiling proudly—and wearing what's left of their army uniforms. This photograph fills the screen until 'An Epitaph to War' finishes.

SCENE FOURTEEN

SHEILA *has just finished packing. She is sitting reading a newspaper when* BRIDIE *enters.*

BRIDIE: [*not really sounding pleased*] Rick's delighted with the show. He's strutting round downstairs like the cat that licked the— [cream]

SHEILA: [*looking at newspaper*] Good. They're predicting fine weather. I hate flying off if there's going to be turbulence.

> SHEILA *stops when she realises that* BRIDIE *is about to lift the suitcase from the bed to the floor.*

Bridie—be careful. You'll do your back. Let me ring the porter—

BRIDIE: And waste ten cents on a tip? Come on—Ichi—ni—san—

> SHEILA *reaches the suitcase just in time to help* BRIDIE.

BOTH: Ya-ta!!

> *And they lower the suitcase to the floor.*

BRIDIE: You should have seen Joyce's suitcase. Three of us had to sit on it for her. [*With some relish*] She stole every sheet and towel in her room—once she found out the Japanese own this place.

SHEILA: [*surprised*] Do they?

> SHEILA *begins to put tea bags, coffee sachets, sugars and motel stationery into her hand bag.* SHEILA *does not steal anything— she just takes all the things that are left out for guests.* BRIDIE, *meanwhile, passes a small sheet of paper to* SHEILA.

BRIDIE: While you're at it—don't forget this.

> SHEILA *glances down at the paper, slightly puzzled.*

My address—and phone number... I thought this time we might try and keep in touch—and not let it go for another fifty years. I might not be around in 2045.

> SHEILA *takes the piece of paper.*

SHEILA: I'll send birthday cards and sugar-free Easter Eggs.

BRIDIE: And what about Christmas?

SHEILA: I was thinking—at Christmas—I might come and feed your chooks.

BRIDIE: [*surprised*] You mean—visit?

SHEILA: Just for a week—if that's not too much trouble.

BRIDIE: [*delighted*] Too much trouble! My dear child—we'll have a proper Christmas dinner—like the ones we always dreamed about—puddings and hams and—

SHEILA: [*searching for something in her handbag*] Not with your cholesterol... Oh, by the way... I think this belongs to you.

SHEILA *holds out the shoe-horn.*

SHEILA: I'm sorry I... kept it so long.

BRIDIE *looks at the shoe-horn, and hesitates.*

Go on. [*Take it.*]

BRIDIE: Are you... sure?

SHEILA: [*firmly*] Of course I'm sure. [*Disapprovingly*] I've never been one for shoe-horns. They stretch the leather and weaken the heels.

BRIDIE *takes the shoe-horn.*

BRIDIE: Oh, Sheila—

BRIDIE *and* SHEILA *hug.*

SHEILA: [*indicating shoe-horn*] Now put that away—or we'll miss our waltz.

BRIDIE: What?

SHEILA: The one you promised me—in Belalau. You distinctly said if the war ever ended, you and I would go dancing.

BRIDIE: You mean now?

SHEILA: At our age it's best not to put things off.

BRIDIE *places the shoe-horn on the small bedside table or on the bed.*

BRIDIE: I... suppose we could... Yes—why not?...

BRIDIE *holds up her arms but* SHEILA *does not move.*

Well—what are you waiting for?

SHEILA: You have to ask me. Properly.

BRIDIE: Why should I ask you?

SHEILA: Because you're the one who made the promise.

BRIDIE: [*sighing*] All right... [*Formally*] Excuse me, Miss Richards. I have heard a somewhat convincing rumour that the Japanese Army has surrendered to the Allies. [*With sincerity*] Which means—I believe—that the war is over. And you and I are free... Would you care to join me in... celebrating peace?

SHEILA: [*slight curtsey*] Thank you. I'd be honoured.

BRIDIE: I suppose you'd rather dance to Frank Sinatra.

SHEILA: At least he knows how to sing in tune.

BRIDIE, *perhaps deliberately, stubs* SHEILA's *toe.*

Ouch! Be careful! Those are my feet you're treading on. You should have let me lead.

BRIDIE: [*tenderly*] Sheila Richards—you're a whinging bloody Pom!

Suddenly the fast and vibrant sequence of Strauss' The Blue Danube starts up loudly—as SHEILA *and* BRIDIE *move off into their waltz.*

As they dance, the stage gradually grows darker and darker— except for a very bright spotlight on BRIDIE*'s shoe-horn.* BRIDIE *and* SHEILA *are confidently dancing and the theatre is filled with Strauss' music. It is the music of joy and triumph and survival.*

THE END